CRANIOGRAPHIC POSITIONING WITH COMPARISON STUDIES

CRANIOGRAPHIC POSITIONING WITH COMPARISON STUDIES

DON Q PARIS, M.A., R.T. (R) (A.R.R.T.)

PROFESSOR AND CHAIRMAN
DEPARTMENT OF MEDICAL RADIOGRAPHY
SCHOOL OF HEALTH PROFESSIONS
NORTHERN ARIZONA UNIVERSITY
FLAGSTAFF, ARIZONA

 F. A. Davis Company · Philadelphia

Library of Congress Cataloging in Publication Data

Paris, Don Q
    Craniographic positioning with comparison studies.

    Bibliography: p.
    Includes index.
    1. Skull—Radiography—Positioning. I. Title.
RC936.P37   1983   617′.51′07572   82-14074
ISBN 0-8036-6768-X

TO MY WIFE, SHERRY;
AND MY CHILDREN, LORI, MARK, JULI, AND BRET Q

PREFACE

The discipline of radiographic positioning is a self-discipline that each individual must master in his or her own way. In order to perfect the "art" and "science" of craniography, the individual must apply a thorough understanding and appreciation of skull anatomy and the relationship of cranial bones in tandem with basic radiographic principles that students learn early in their training. Positioning all skulls with the same degree of head manipulation to demonstrate areas of the petrous region, for instance, can only result in many repeat examinations and register despair on the faces of many radiologists. Applying a learned knowledge of cephalic measurements and indexing enables the radiographer to perform, with personal satisfaction, many skull procedures that have heretofore been passed on or left for a chosen few to complete.

In addition to perfecting the technical art of craniography, the health professional must adopt the positive attitude and self-pride that each procedure must be "all-inclusive" in providing the radiologist with a series of radiographs that will enhance a correct diagnosis and minimize areas to question. To adopt the principle that "borderline" radiographs can pass as satisfactory is tantamount to jeopardizing a patient's health, to say nothing of the performance rating that will precede the radiographer to many employers.

The major function or purpose of a radiographic positioning text should be to provide precise, explicit information that will lead the reader to an early conclusion. The unique design of this textbook is not only to provide precise instruction for routine craniographic positioning, but also to graphically illustrate how modifications from the correct alignments will change the anatomic structures under consideration. In some instances, the modifications will enhance viewing of certain anatomic structures worthy of special consideration. However, the main purpose of each modification is to provide a "blueprint" or comparison view to determine what manipulations are necessary to correct the position when a routine radiographic view appears to be malaligned and the patient should be repositioned.

No attempt has been made in this publication to illustrate, or provide instructions for, the use of sophisticated equipment or special skull procedures, owing to the wide variety that may be applied throughout the country. It is felt that when a radiographer has mastered the many routine positioning procedures, the procedures can then be applied effectively to any special circumstance as required.

The book begins with an easy-to-understand review of medical terminology and anatomic nomenclature of the cranium, followed by guideline and landmark definitions, which are provided for proper association with each position. Detailed instruction on how to determine and classify cranial shapes for accurate positioning of the petrosal region comprises the balance of the prepositioning units.

Each correct routine position in this publication demonstrates the related anatomic structures and is accompanied by two comparison studies to show anatomic changes, along with corrective measures.

It has been said that the quality of an education can be determined by how effectively it can be applied. It is the intent of this book to provide the sequential instruction that will assist the reader in perfecting a specialized health skill. Yours is a highly valued science and a responsibility that directly affects a patient's well-being. Learn your lessons well.

Don Q Paris

ACKNOWLEDGMENTS

The value of most textbooks can largely be determined by the clarity and accuracy of the illustrations therein. I gratefully acknowledge the invaluable contribution of all of the artistic drawings in this textbook, which were prepared by my very talented daughter, Juli L. Martineau, Flagstaff, Arizona.

It is with appreciation that I acknowledge the encouragement and technical expertise extended to me by Richard Foust, Ph.D., of Northern Arizona University. His mastery of photographic principles and techniques has been applied extensively in the development of this textbook.

To Rosemary Anderson, my secretary, I extend my sincere thanks for her considerable assistance in the professional preparation of the entire textbook manuscript.

Lee Thorsell, B.S.R.T., Instructor and Department Photographer; and Peter Marks, B.S.M.R., and Renaldo Jacques, B.S.M.R., radiographers, contributed a considerable amount of time in the preparation of materials for this publication, which I deeply appreciate.

To Robert G. Martone, Allied Health Editor, and the staff of F. A. Davis Company, I wish to express my gratitude and thanks for all their assistance throughout the preparation of this book.

A long-time friend and pioneer in radiologic technology education, Charles A. Jacobi, B.Sc., R.T., Professor Emeritus, was instrumental in introducing me to the teaching and writing professions. His initial inspiration and encouragement are reflected in the development of this textbook and will always be appreciated.

During the preparation of this textbook, I have received from my wife, Sherry, both encouragement and helpful criticism, for which I will always be most grateful.

DQP

CONTENTS

UNIT 5   SINUS POSITIONING

UNIT 6   FACIAL BONE POSITIONING   113

SKULL ANATOMY

UNIT 1

TERMINOLOGY

The skeletal system is divided into two general sections called the appendicular and the axial skeleton. A major component of the axial skeleton is the skull, consisting of a cranial vault (8 separate bones) and facial bones (14 separate bones), for a total of 22 bones. To promote better understanding of the language of skull anatomy, the following terminology is provided for review:

acoustic. Pertaining to the sense or organs of hearing, to sound, or to the science of sounds; auditory.

ala. A wing or wing-like process or part, as the alae of the nose, of the vomer.

alveolar. Pertaining to the part of the mandibular and maxillary ridges where the sockets for the teeth are situated. Pertaining to the air cells of the lungs.

anterior. Situated in front of or in the forward part of the body. Opposed to posterior. Same as ventral in the trunk region.

antrum. A cavern, cavity, or sinus, known as the maxillary sinus in the maxillary bone.

apex. The tip, point, or angular summit of anything; a vertex. As the apex nasi, the tip of the nose.

apophysis. A process of a bone that has never been entirely separated from the bone of which it forms a part.

arch. A structural member, usually curved and made up of separate wedge-shaped solids, with their joints at right angles to the curve. To form or bend into the shape of an arch.

asterion. The point of union of the occipital, parietal, and temporal bones on the surface of the skull.

auricular. Auricle, the external ear; pertaining to the ear or sense of hearing.

basalis. The base of the skull.

basilar. Pertaining to a base or basal part. Relating to or situated at the base.

basion. The middle of the anterior margin of the foramen magnum.

brain. The large mass of nerve tissue enclosed in the skull or cranium, in which the anterior end of the spinal cord terminates.

bregma. The point on the surface of the skull at the junction of the coronal and sagittal sutures.

calvaria. Domelike upper part of the cranium.

canal. A duct, tubular passage.

canthus. The corner on each side of the eye where the upper and lower eyelids meet. Also known as the commissure.

carotid. The principal artery of the neck, or near such artery or arteries.

caudal. Near the tail or hind part of the body.

cephalad. Toward the head end of the body. Opposite of caudal.

cerebrum. The main portion of the brain occupying the upper part of the cranium.

choana. Any funnel-shaped cavity, or infundibulum.

cleft. A space or opening made by splitting. A crack or fissure.

clinoid. Hornlike. Resembling bed posts. Processes of the sphenoid bone on the superior surface.

commissure. The corner on each side of the eye where the upper and lower eyelids meet. Also known as the canthus.

condyloid. Shaped like, pertaining to, or situated near a condyle.

cornu. The middle turbinate bone; hornlike.

coronal. A suture extending across the skull between the parietal and frontal bones.

coronoid. The process of the ramus of the lower jaw, to which the temporal and part of the masseter muscles are attached.

cranium. The skull of a vertebrate.

crest. A projecting ridge.

cribriform. The horizontal plate of the ethmoid bone, perforated with numerous foramina for the passage of the olfactory nerve filaments from the cranial to the nasal cavity.

crista galli. An upwardly directed median triangular process of the ethmoid bone to which the falx cerebri is attached.

cuspid. A canine tooth.

dorsum. Same as posterior. Opposed to anterior or front.

duct. Any tube, canal, or vessel; usually applied to those that carry off the secretion of a gland.

ear. The organ of hearing, containing the external, middle, and internal parts.

eminence. A prominence or projection, especially one on the surface of a bone.

encephalograph. A radiograph made after injecting air into the spinal canal; the air rises and defines the sinuses of the brain.

ethmoid. Designating one or more bones forming part of the walls and septum of the nasal cavity. The ethmoid bone or the sinuses contained therein.

external. Situated or occurring on the outside of the body; away from the median plane. Opposite of internal.

eye. The organ of sight.

facial. Of or pertaining to the face.

floor. The bottom.

fontanel, fontanelle. Any one of the unossified spots on the cranium of a young infant.

foramen magnum. The opening in the base of the occipital bone through which the spinal canal passes.

fossa. A pit or depression, as the temporal fossa of the skull.

frontal. Of or pertaining to the forehead, as the frontal bone.

glabella. The smooth prominence between the eyebrows.

hamulus. Any hook-shaped process.

head. The end of anything considered the upper end or the top.

helix. The incurved rim of the external ear.

hiatus. An opening, a gap, a break with a part missing.

hyoid. Designating or pertaining to a U-shaped bone or bones at the base of the tongue.

hypophysis. The pituitary body.

incisor. Any of the cutting teeth in front of the canines in either jaw.

inferior. Underneath or situated lower. Opposite of superior.

infraorbital. Beneath the orbit or eye socket.

infundibulum. Any of various funnel-shaped or dilated organs or parts, as the hollow conical process of gray matter to which the pituitary body is attached.

inion. The center of the external occipital protuberance of the skull.

jugular. Of or pertaining to the throat or neck, as the jugular vein.

lacrimal. Of or pertaining to tears. Designating, pertaining to, or situated near the organs producing tears.

lambda. The point of junction of the sagittal and lambdoid sutures of the skull.

lambdoid. A suture extending across the skull between the parietal and occipital bones.

lateral. Of or pertaining to the side. Away from the medial plane. Opposed to medial.

lid. That which covers the opening. The cover for the eye.

lingual. Of or pertaining to the tongue or a tongue-like organ or part.

lip. Either of the two fleshy folds that surround the orifice of the mouth in humans and many animals.

lobe. A projection or division of a somewhat rounded form. The lobes of the brain or ears.

magnum. Great or large.

malar. Pertaining to the cheek or side of the head. The malar bone, known as the zygomatic bone.

mandible. The bone of the lower jaw.

mastoid. Nipple-shaped. The mastoid process of the temporal bone, sometimes called the mastoid bone.

maxillary. Pertaining to the upper, or superior, jaw bones (paired).

meatus. A natural passage or canal. The opening of such a passage.

medial. Being situated or occurring in the middle of the body. Median, mesial.

meningeal. Pertaining to the three membranes (the dura mater, arachnoid, and pia mater) that envelop the brain and spinal cord.

mental. Pertaining to the chin or lower jaw.

molar. Having power to grind. Of or pertaining to the molar teeth situated behind the incisors and canines.

nasal. Of or pertaining to the nose.

nasion. The midpoint of the nasofrontal suture.

neck. The part connecting the head and trunk or body.

norma. A line established to define aspects of the cranium.

notch. A V-shaped indentation; a nick. A depression, chiefly one on the edge of a bone.

nuchal. The back, nape, or scruff of the neck.

obelion. A point on the sagittal suture where it is crossed by a line that connects the parietal foramina.

occipital. The posterior part of the skull. The occipital bone.

occiput. The back part of the skull.

opisthion. The midpoint of the lower posterior border of the foramen magnum.

opisthocranion. Most posterior point on the external surface of the occipital bone.

optic. Of or pertaining to vision of the eye.

orbit. The eye socket.

palatine. Of or pertaining to the palate. The palatine bones.

palpebral. Of or pertaining to the eyelids.

parietal. Of or pertaining to the parietes, or walls, of a part or cavity. The parietal bones of the skull.

parotid. The salivary gland inferior and anterior to the ear. The parotid gland.

petrous. Designating or pertaining to the exceptionally hard and dense medial portion of the temporal bone containing the internal auditory organs.

philtrum. The groove at the medial line of the upper lip.

pinna. The upper part of the external ear.

pituitary. Pertaining to a small, oval, two-lobed vascular body attached to the infundibulum of the brain and seated in the sella turcica. The pituitary gland.

plate. A smooth, flat piece of material of uniform thickness.

posterior. Situated behind or toward the rear. Opposed to anterior. Same as dorsal.

process. Any marked prominence or projecting part; an outgrowth or extension.

protuberance. That which bulges beyond the surrounding or adjacent surface; swelling, a prominence; an elevation.

pterion. The juncture of the frontal and parietal bones with the great wing of the sphenoid.

pterygoid. A process extending downward from each side of the sphenoid bone, consisting of two vertical plates, the internal and external, separated by an angular (pterygoid) notch and so placed as to leave a deep (pterygoid) fossa on its outer and posterior aspect.

ramus. The ascending branch at each end of the lower jawbone.

raphe. A ridge or furrow that marks the line of union of the halves of symmetric parts. The middle ridge of the palate.

roof. The top or summit.

sagittal. The suture between the parietal bones of the skull, dividing the human into right and left portions; or any line parallel thereto.

sella. A seat-shaped fossa or depression, such as the sella turcica, the pituitary fossa.

septum. Any dividing wall, or partition, separating two cavities or masses. The nasal septum, separating the two nasal cavities.

sinciput. The forehead; the upper half of the skull.

sinus. A cavity, recess, or depression. An air cavity in the cranial bones.

skull. The skeleton of the head. The bony framework that encloses and protects the brain and chief sense organs. The 8 cranial bones and the 14 facial bones.

sphenoid. Designating or pertaining to a wedge or winged, compound bone of the base of the cranium.

spine. A stiff, sharp-pointed process.

squamous. The anterior, upper portion of the temporal bone.

stephanion. The point where the coronal suture crosses the superior temporal ridge.

styloid. Resembling a pen, or stylus, long and pointed.

sub. Under, below, beneath, or lower.

sulcus. A shallow furrow on the surface of the brain, separating convolutions. The furrow between the lower lip and the chin, between the nose and upper lip.

superciliary. Pertaining to the eyebrow; supraorbital ridge.

superior. Above or situated higher. Opposed to inferior.

supraorbital. Above the orbit of the eye.

suture. The line of union, or seam, in an immovable articulation, such as those between the bones of the skull.

temporal. Of or pertaining to the temple or temples or the sides of the skull behind the orbits.

tragus. The prominence anterior to the external opening of the ear.

transverse. Lying or being across; crosswise.

tubercle. A protuberance.

turcica. Sella turcica, the pituitary fossa.

tympanic. Of or pertaining to the tympanum, eardrum, or hearing.

velum. Any veil or veil-like organ. The pendulous and posterior portion of the soft palate.

ventricle. Any small cavity; any one of the various cavities of the brain.

ventriculography. Radiography of the brain following the direct injection of air into the cerebral ventricles. Employed in the diagnosis of brain tumors.

vertex. The top of the head. The summit or crown.

vertical. Of or pertaining to the vertex; situated at the vertex, or highest point. Perpendicular to the horizon.

vesicle. A small sac containing fluid.

vomer. A bone of the skull situated below the ethmoidal region, forming part of the nasal septum.

wing. Resembling the wing, or organ of aerial flight. The greater and lesser wings of the sphenoid bone.

zygomatic. The zygomatic, or malar, bone of the face. The cheekbone.

CRANIAL BONES (8)

Bones that comprise the cranial vault or brain case are:

Frontal (single): anterior superior wall and anterior floor.

Parietal (paired): superior and lateral and upper posterior walls.

Occipital (single): lower posterior wall and central posterior floor.

Temporal (paired): lateral walls and central floor.

Sphenoid (single): anterior lateral walls and central floor.

Ethmoid (single): anterior central floor.

FACIAL BONES (14)

Bones that comprise the facial region are:

Nasal (paired): superior, bridge of nose.

Lacrimal (paired): smallest facial bone; medial margin of bony eye orbit.

Zygomatic (paired): lateral margin and wall of bony eye orbit; malar, or cheek, bone.

Maxillae (paired): upper jaw, anterior roof of hard palate, and anterior walls and floor of nasal cavity.

Palatine (paired): posterior roof of hard palate, and posterior walls and floor of nasal cavity.

Vomer (single): posterior partition of nasal septum.

Inferior nasal concha (paired): attached to maxillary bone on the wall of nasal cavity.

Mandible (single): largest facial bone; lower jaw.

SKULL REGIONS

Anterior View (Fig. 1-1)

The anterior view consists of six regions: frontal, zygomatic, nasal, orbital, maxillary, and mandibular.

FRONTAL REGION. The superior **ala,** or smooth **sinciput,** forms the forehead, articulating superiorly with the **parietal** bones by the **coronal** suture. The anterior surfaces, **frontal eminences,** are located above the **superciliary arches,** which are above the orbits. The **supraorbital margins** articulate medially with the nasal bones and laterally with the zygomatic bones. The **supraorbital notch,** which transmits the supraorbital nerve and vessels, is found in the medial supraorbital margin. The **glabella,** a raised area between the **superciliary arches,** is a major palpation point for many skull positions and for locating the frontal sinus. A reference point at the superior junction of the nasal bones and the frontal bone is called the **nasion.** The frontal bone projects posteriorly at the supraorbital margins to form the roof of the orbits and anterior floor of the cranial vault.

ZYGOMATIC REGION. The **malar,** or cheek, bone forms the lateral floor, wall, and margins of the orbital cavity. The **temporal process** extends posteriorly to articulate with the **zygomatic process** of the temporal bone to form the **zygomatic arch.**

NASAL REGION. The nasal bones articulate together by the **intranasal suture** in line with the midsagittal plane. They articulate superiorly with the frontal bone and laterally with the frontal processes of the maxillary bone. The inferior margins of the nasal bones form the anterior **nasal antrum,** along with the **nasal septum** and the medial walls of the **maxillae.** The **inferior nasal conchae** bones may be located inside the lower lateral margins of the anterior nasal aperture.

ORBITAL REGION. The concave, bony eye orbit is formed by the **frontal, sphenoid,** and **ethmoid** (three cranial) bones and the **zygo-**matic, **maxillary, lacrimal,** and **palatine** (four facial) bones. In the posteromedial aspect is the **optic foramen;** posterosuperior, the **superior orbital fissure;** and posteroinferior, the **inferior orbital fissure** and **infraorbital groove** that transmits to the **infraorbital foramen.** On the anteromedial margin is the **lacrimal fossa,** which houses the tear duct.

MAXILLARY REGION. The maxillae house the largest of the paranasal sinuses and extend the **frontal processes** superiorly to articulate with the frontal bone. The maxillary bone forms the lateral wall of the **nasal antrum,** the inferomedial margin, and floor of the bony eye orbit. The **infraorbital foramen** is found on the anterior surface, and the **zygomatic process** extends laterally to articulate with the zygomatic bone. The maxilla ends inferiorly as the **alveolar process,** which houses the upper teeth. The **acanthion,** tip of the **anterior nasal spine,** is found at the inferomedial margin of the anterior nasal aperture.

MANDIBULAR REGION. The largest of the facial bones, the mandible, joins its halves together at the anterior midline to form the **symphysis menti** and terminates inferiorly into a slight eminence called the **mental protuberance.** The **alveolar process** runs along the superior margin of the mandibular body and houses the lower teeth. The **mental foramen,** located in the anterior, center one third of the body, is in line with the second premolar and transmits the mental branch of the mandibular nerve and mental vessels.

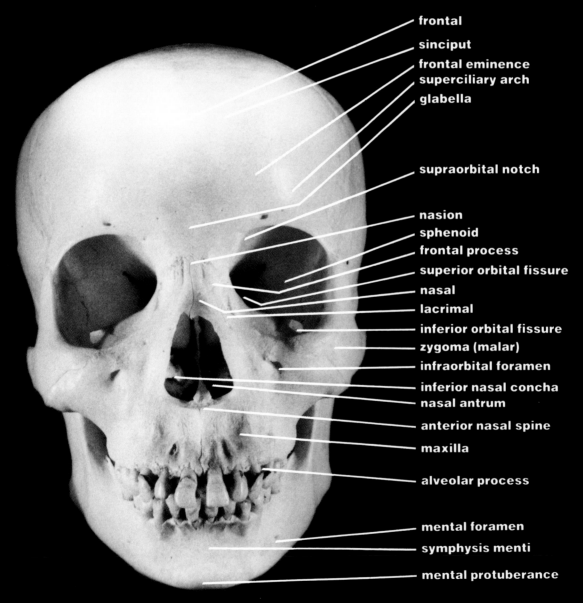

frontal
sinciput
frontal eminence
superciliary arch
glabella

supraorbital notch

nasion
sphenoid
frontal process
superior orbital fissure
nasal
lacrimal
inferior orbital fissure
zygoma (malar)
infraorbital foramen
inferior nasal concha
nasal antrum
anterior nasal spine
maxilla

alveolar process

mental foramen
symphysis menti
mental protuberance

FIGURE 1-1. Skull, anterior aspect.

Lateral View (Fig. 1-2)

The lateral view consists primarily of the occipital, parietal, frontal, temporal, and sphenoid components of the cranial vault. Nasal, lacrimal, zygomatic, maxillary, and mandibular facial bones constitute the other bones visualized in the lateral aspect.

CRANIAL VAULT. The **coronal suture** is found approximately in the middle, separating the frontal from the parietal bones. At the junction of the **squamosal suture** and the posterosuperior point of the greater sphenoid wing is a reference point called the **pterion.** The **asterion,** another reference point, is found at the junction of the **parietomastoid, lambdoidal,** and **occipitomastoid sutures.** Posteriorly, the lambdoidal suture separates the narrow silhouette of the occiput from the parietal bones and continues inferiorly as the **occipitomastoid suture** beyond the junction of the squamosal suture.

The **squamous portion** of the temporal bone is distinguished anteriorly from the **great wing** of the **sphenoid** by the sphenosquamosal suture, and superiorly from the parietals by the **squamosal suture.** The temporal bone terminates inferiorly into the **mastoid process.** Anterior and adjacent to the mastoid is the tympanic portion, which houses the **external auditory meatus.** The tip of the **styloid process** can be seen extended slightly anteriorly and inferiorly from the medial side of the tympanic portion. The temporal bone extends a **zygomatic process** anteriorly to articulate with the **temporal process** of the zygomatic bone to form the total **zygomatic arch.**

The greater wing of the sphenoid, posterior to the zygomatic bone within the temporal fossa, articulates with temporal, parietal, frontal, and zygomatic bones.

FACIAL REGION. The zygomatic (malar) bone extends a **frontal process** superiorly to articulate with the **zygomatic process** of the frontal bone.

The maxilla is inferior to the zygomatic bone, extending both posteriorly and anteriorly, with the superior projection of the **frontal process** separating lateral views of the **nasal** and **lacrimal** bones. The **zygomatic process** extends superiorly and laterally to articulate with the **maxillary** process of the zygomatic bone.

The mandible clearly defines its **body, alveolar process,** lower portion of the **coronoid process, semilunar (mandibular) notch, condyle, ramus,** and **mandibular angle.**

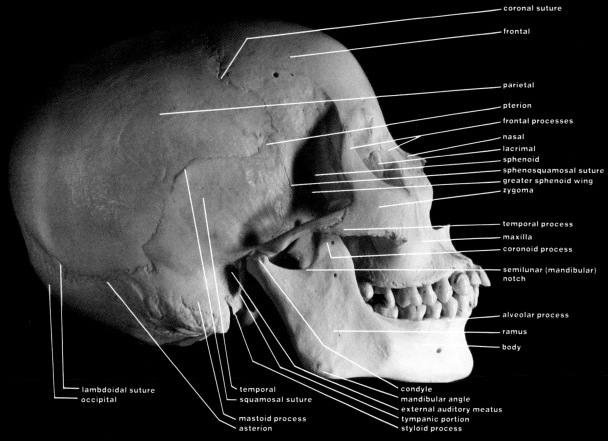

coronal suture

frontal

parietal

pterion

frontal processes

nasal

lacrimal

sphenoid

sphenosquamosal suture

greater sphenoid wing

zygoma

temporal process

maxilla

coronoid process

semilunar (mandibular) notch

alveolar process

ramus

body

lambdoidal suture

occipital

temporal

squamosal suture

mastoid process

asterion

condyle

mandibular angle

external auditory meatus

tympanic portion

styloid process

FIGURE 1-2. Skull, lateral aspect.

Basal View (Fig. 1-3)

The basal view consists of two general regions, the anterior and the posterior.

ANTERIOR REGION. The hard palate, arched by the alveolar process with erupting teeth, is formed by the **palatine process** of the maxilla and the **horizontal plate** of palatine bones. The **median palatine suture** connects with the **incisive foramen** in the anterior midline and with the **posterior nasal spine** in the posterior midline. Superior to this spine is the plow-shaped **vomer** bone, which forms the posteromedian partition or **septum.** The two **choanae,** or posterior nasal apertures, are separated by the vomer and surrounded laterally by the **medial pterygoid plates.** The **pterygoid fossa** is found between the plates on either side, with the medial pterygoid plate terminating inferiorly as the **hamulus process.** Extending laterally from the base of the pterygoid plate is the sphenoid bone. Located in a posterolateral line from the base of the lateral plate are the **foramen ovale** and the smaller **foramen spinosum.**

The inferior aspect very well demonstrates the zygomatic arch with its connections to the zygomatic and temporal bones. The depressions at the posterior base of the arches are the mandibular fossae.

POSTERIOR REGION. The basilar part of the occiput joins the posterior surface of the sphenoid at about the middle of the cranial floor. To either side of this union is an irregular opening, the **foramen lacerum,** that is formed by the great wing of the sphenoid, the apex of the petrous portion of the temporal bone, and the basilar part of the occipital bone. Posterolateral is the **carotid orifice,** which is interconnected to the **foramen lacerum** by the **carotid canal.** Continuing in the same posterolateral line, the **styloid process, stylomastoid foramen,** and **mastoid tip** are all detected within the base of the temporal bone.

Posterior to the carotid foramen, the irregular **jugular foramen** is formed by the temporal and occipital bones.

On both sides of the foramen magnum are two elevated, articular surfaces called the **oc-cipital condyles.** The **condyloid fossa** is located at the posterior base of the condyle. At the anterior base of the condyle is the **hypoglossal canal** whose origin is found within the lateral margin of the foramen magnum. The **basion** and **opisthion** are reference points located respectively on the anterior and posterior aspects of the **foramen magnum.**

Extending posteriorly from the opisthion is the external occipital crest, which comes together with the superior nuchal line in a raised area called the **external occipital protuberance** (EOP) whose center point is referred to as the inion.

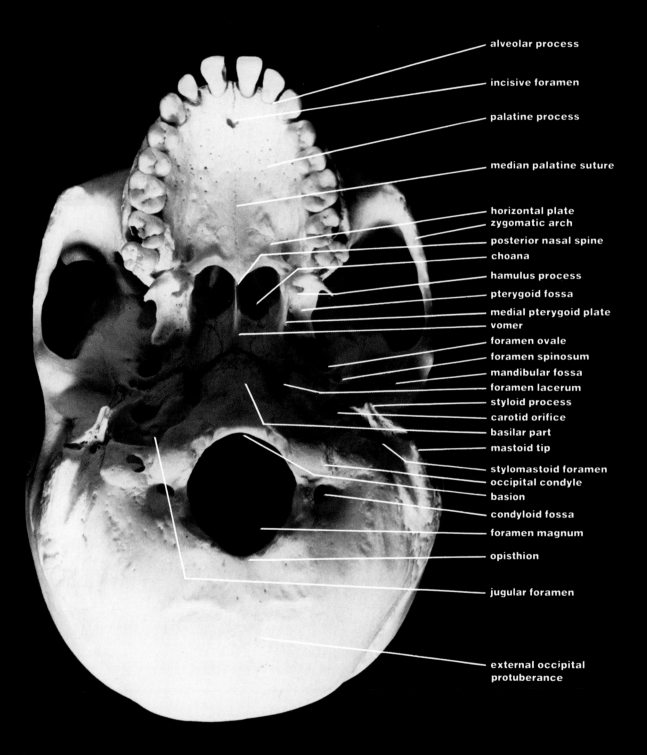

alveolar process

incisive foramen

palatine process

median palatine suture

horizontal plate
zygomatic arch
posterior nasal spine
choana
hamulus process
pterygoid fossa
medial pterygoid plate
vomer
foramen ovale
foramen spinosum
mandibular fossa
foramen lacerum
styloid process
carotid orifice
basilar part
mastoid tip

stylomastoid foramen
occipital condyle
basion
condyloid fossa
foramen magnum

opisthion

jugular foramen

external occipital
protuberance

FIGURE 1-3. Skull, basilar aspect.

Cranial View (Fig. 1-4)

Three fossae are designated within the cranial cavity: anterior, middle, and posterior.

ANTERIOR FOSSA. The anterior fossa is located within the internal perimeters of the frontal bone and is bounded posteriorly by the **lesser wings** of the **sphenoid.** The frontal crest is a sharply defined ridge extending from the anterior floor, superiorly in the midline of the frontal bone. At the base of the crest are the **cribriform plates** of the ethmoid bone (perforated for transmission of olfactory nerves) that are partitioned by the **crista galli** (cock's comb).

MIDDLE FOSSA. The middle fossa is designed with two lateral depressions that contain the temporal lobes of the brain. A sculptured central elevation, the **pituitary fossa,** is bordered anteriorly by the lesser wings of the sphenoid and the chiasmatic ridge; laterally by the great wings of the sphenoid, parietals, and squamae of the temporals; and posteriorly by the dorsum sellae and the petrous portion of the temporal bones.

Within the lesser wings of the sphenoid are located the **optic foramina,** with connecting **chiasmatic groove** and adjacent **tuberculum sellae.** The **anterior clinoid processes** are posterior terminations of the lesser wings. The deep depression just posterior to the **tuberculum sellae** is the **sella turcica** (Turkish saddle), or hypophyseal fossa, which seats the pituitary gland. Posterior to the sella turcica is the **dorsum sellae,** terminating on both sides as **posterior clinoid processes.** Sloping inferiorly from either side of the sella turcica to line up with the superomedial outlet of the **foramen lacerum** is the **carotid sulcus.**

Within the lateral depression, anterior to and directly beneath the anterior clinoid process is the **foramen rotundum.** Laterally adjacent to the foramen lacerum are the **foramen ovale** and smaller associate, the **foramen spinosum.**

The superior border of the **petrous portion** is known as the **ridge,** with the highest point designated the **arcuate eminence.**

POSTERIOR FOSSA. The deepest fossa contains the cerebellum and pons and projects the medulla oblongata through the centralized **foramen magnum.**

The basilar part of the occiput extends anterosuperiorly from the foramen magnum to join the dorsum sellae. Inside the lateral border of the foramen is the **hypoglossal canal.** Lateral to the canal, at the base of the petrous portion, is the irregularly shaped **jugular foramen;** and just superior, on the posterior surface of the petrous wall, is the **internal acoustic meatus.**

The **transverse sinus** and the **superior sagittal sinus** join at an elevated point in the midline to define the **internal occipital protuberance.**

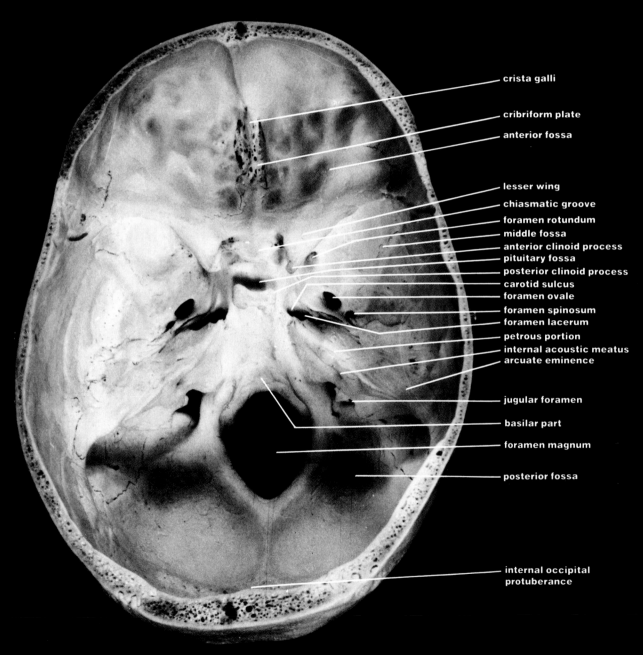

crista galli

cribriform plate

anterior fossa

lesser wing

chiasmatic groove

foramen rotundum

middle fossa

anterior clinoid process

pituitary fossa

posterior clinoid process

carotid sulcus

foramen ovale

foramen spinosum

foramen lacerum

petrous portion

internal acoustic meatus

arcuate eminence

jugular foramen

basilar part

foramen magnum

posterior fossa

internal occipital
protuberance

FIGURE 1-4. Skull, cranial aspect.

Orbital Cavity, Anterior Oblique View (Fig. 1-5)

The funnel-shaped concavity is designed so as to present a medial wall, lateral wall, roof, floor, base, and apex; the apex is centered when the bony eye orbit is placed in the anterior oblique position. The bony eye orbit, per se, is composed of seven bones: **frontal, sphenoid, palatine, ethmoid, lacrimal, maxillary,** and **zygomatic.**

MEDIAL WALL. Both medial walls are situated nearly parallel on each side of the ethmoid sinuses. Each medial wall includes the frontal process of the maxillary, the lacrimal, the lamina of the ethmoid, a small segment of the sphenoid body, and the orbital process of the frontal bone.

LATERAL WALL. The lateral wall includes the orbital process of the zygomatic and the orbital (anterior) surface of the sphenoid.

ROOF. The roof includes the orbital plate of the frontal and the lesser wing of the sphenoid.

FLOOR. The floor includes the orbital surface of the zygomatic, the maxilla, and the small orbital process of the palatine.

BASE. The base is formed by the orbital margin, which includes the frontal, maxilla, and zygomatic bones.

APEX. The apex terminates in the optic foramen, which is housed within the lesser wing of the sphenoid.

In addition to the **optic foramen,** the superior and inferior orbital fissures are diagnostic areas of concern. The **superior orbital fissure** is located toward the apex of the orbit and conforms to a wedge-shaped slit extending superiorly and laterally. The **inferior orbital fissure** is located in the posterior floor of the orbit and conforms to a wedge-shaped slit extending anteriorly and laterally.

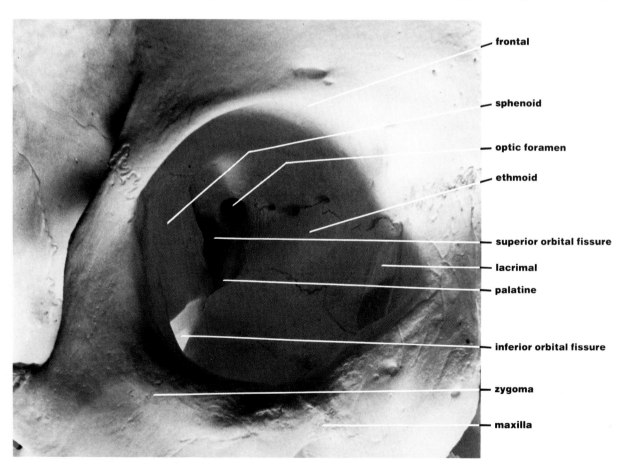

frontal

sphenoid

optic foramen

ethmoid

superior orbital fissure

lacrimal

palatine

inferior orbital fissure

zygoma

maxilla

FIGURE 1-5. Orbital cavity, anterior aspect.

Nasal Cavity, Midsagittal View (Fig. 1-6)

Each of the two parts of the nasal cavity is formed by a medial and lateral wall, a roof, and a floor. An anterior opening, the nasal aperture, communicates through a funnel-shaped passageway to the posterior opening, the choana.

MEDIAL WALL. Formed by the crests of the maxillae and palatine bones, the vomer, the rostrum of the sphenoid, and crest of the ethmoid, the medial wall, or the **nasal septum,** separates the nasal cavity into two parts. In addition to jointly using the medial wall, each cavity is formed by the following:

LATERAL WALL. Six bones make up the lateral wall: the **lacrimal, maxilla, inferior nasal concha, ethmoid, sphenoid,** and **palatine.**

ROOF. The six bones that form the roof are the **frontal, nasal, ethmoid, sphenoid, vomer,** and **palatine.**

FLOOR. The **horizontal plate** of the **palatine** joins the **palatine process** of the **maxilla** at the **palatomaxillary suture** to form the floor in each part of the nasal cavity.

The **superior concha,** which can be visualized through the choana with a superior angle, and the **middle concha** are processes of the ethmoid bone. The **inferior concha** (turbinate) bone is attached to the maxillary portion of the lateral wall.

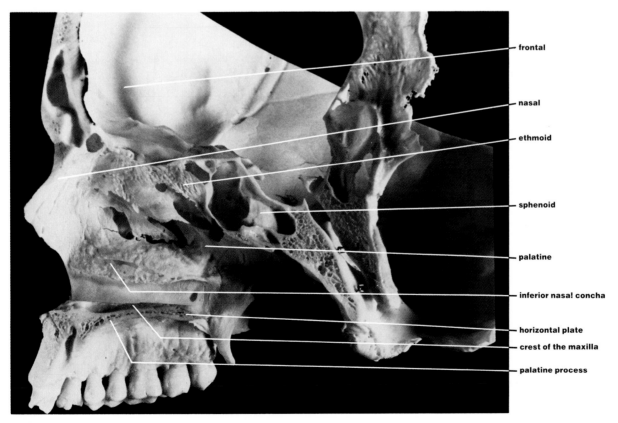

frontal

nasal

ethmoid

sphenoid

palatine

inferior nasal concha

horizontal plate

crest of the maxilla

palatine process

FIGURE 1-6. Facial region, midsagittal aspect.

Paranasal Sinuses, Anterior Oblique View (Fig. 1-7)

The four named paranasal sinuses of radiographic consideration are the **frontal** (one, divided), **ethmoid** (two clusters), **sphenoid** (one, divided), and the **maxillary,** or antra of Highmore (two).

FRONTAL. Usually of cauliflower design, the frontal sinus is located within the frontal bone posterior to the **glabella.** It communicates with the nasal cavity via the frontonasal duct. Occasionally, the frontal sinus may not be demonstrated radiographically on some patients because of lack of cavity formation.

ETHMOID. Located superiorly and posteriorly within the ethmoid bone, the small **ethmoid sinuses** are separated by the nasal septum and bounded laterally by the medial orbital wall. They are usually classified into anterior and posterior groups, with the former draining into the **infundibulum** and the latter draining beneath the **superior concha** into the nasal cavity.

SPHENOID. Situated within the sphenoid body, inferior to the sella turcica, the **sphenoid sinus** drains into the **sphenoethmoidal recess** via the sphenopalatine foramen.

MAXILLARY. Occasionally referred to as the antra of Highmore, the **maxillary** are the largest of the paranasal sinuses. They occupy the space within the maxillae, lateral to the nasal cavity, inferior to the orbital floor, and superior to the alveolar arch. The upper molar roots are close enough to occasionally penetrate the antrum floor in some patients. The sinus drains into the **semilunar hiatus** of the nasal cavity.

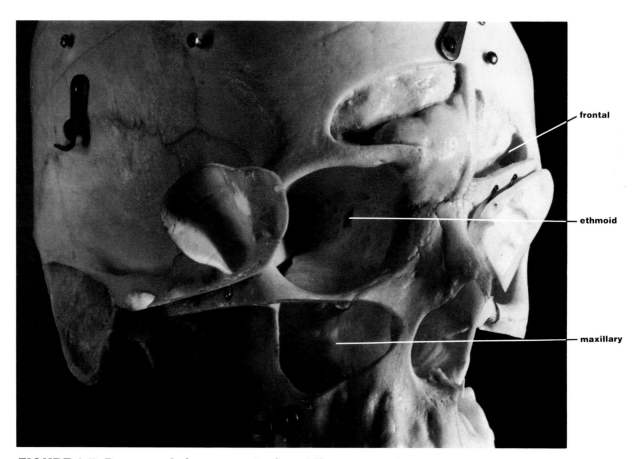

frontal

ethmoid

maxillary

FIGURE 1-7. Paranasal sinuses, anterior-oblique aspect.

INDIVIDUAL CRANIAL BONES

It is important to study the cranial bones in their relationship with each other as well as separately in order to better understand and correctly critique the resulting radiographic views. Therefore, helpful comments will be made periodically to assist the reader in associating anatomic landmarks and reference points with the skull regions illustrated in Figures 1-1 through 1-4.

Frontal Bone
(Figs. 1-8 and 1-9)

As viewed from the lateral aspect, the frontal bone forms a curved angle or L shape; therefore, it exhibits two portions: the squama or forehead, and the orbital or horizontal.

SQUAMA OR FOREHEAD, ANTERIOR VIEW (FIG. 1-8)

Frontal Eminence. Anterior surface, on each side of median line, superior to the supraorbital ridge.

Superciliary Arches. Elevated ridges on each side of median line, about halfway between frontal eminence and supraorbital ridges.

Glabella. Raised area between the superciliary arches. Palpation point for locating the frontal sinus.

Supraorbital Ridges (Margins). Superior border of bony eye orbit.

Supraorbital Notch (Foramen). Superior-center margin of supraorbital ridge.

Zygomatic Process. Anterolateral point of supraorbital ridge.

Nasion. Center point of articulation with nasal bones.

Nasal Spine. A sharp-pointed process projecting inferiorly from beneath the frontal sinus to articulate with the perpendicular plate of the ethmoid to help form the nasal septum.

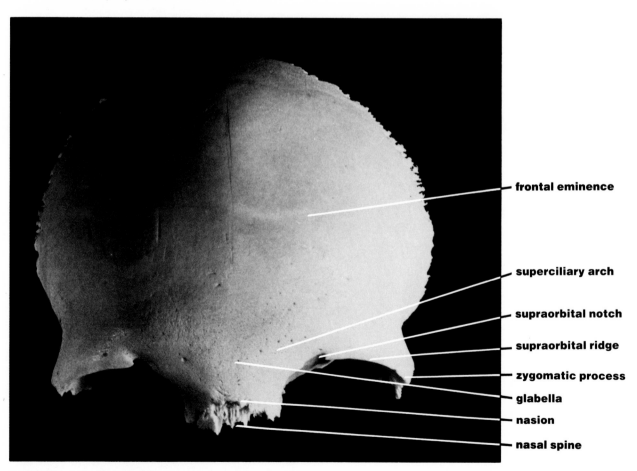

— frontal eminence

— superciliary arch

— supraorbital notch

— supraorbital ridge

— zygomatic process

— glabella

— nasion

— nasal spine

FIGURE 1-8. Frontal bone, external aspect.

ORBITAL OR HORIZONTAL, INFERIOR VIEW (FIG. 1-9)

Orbital Plates. Form each roof of the orbital cavities on the inferior surfaces.

Ethmoidal Notch. A depression between the two orbital plates that contains the horizontal cribriform plate of the ethmoid.

Frontal Sinuses. Anterior and superior to the ethmoidal notch; they are divided by a thin, central membrane, and extend laterally within the frontal bone.

The seven named bones that articulate with the frontal bone are three cranial bones, the **parietal** (two), **sphenoid** (one), and **ethmoid** (one); and four facial bones, the **zygomatic** (two), **maxilla** (two), **lacrimal** (two), and **nasal** (two).

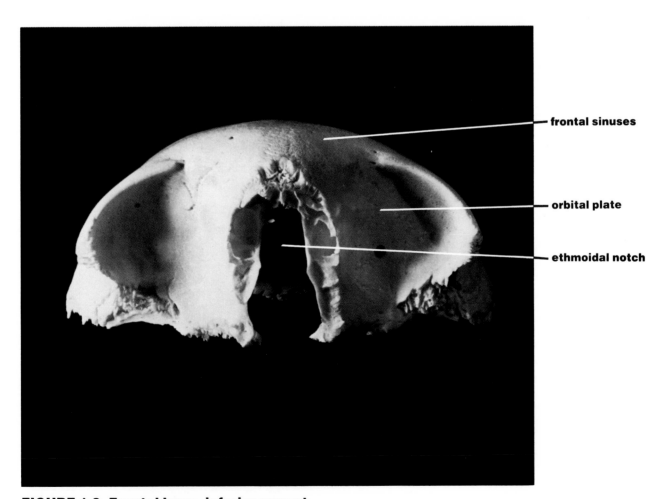

— frontal sinuses

— orbital plate

— ethmoidal notch

FIGURE 1-9. Frontal bone, inferior aspect.

Parietal Bone (Figs. 1-10 and 1-11)

Forming the posterolateral portion of the calvarium, the two sections of the parietal bone join at the vertex to create the sagittal suture.

EXTERNAL SURFACE (FIG. 1-10)

Parietal Foramen. On each side of the sagittal suture, approximately 3.5 cm superior to the junction of the sagittal and lambdoidal sutures (lambda).

Temporal Lines. Ossification lines (superior and inferior) separating the upper, smooth parietal eminence from the lower, narrower temporalis that articulates with the temporal squama.

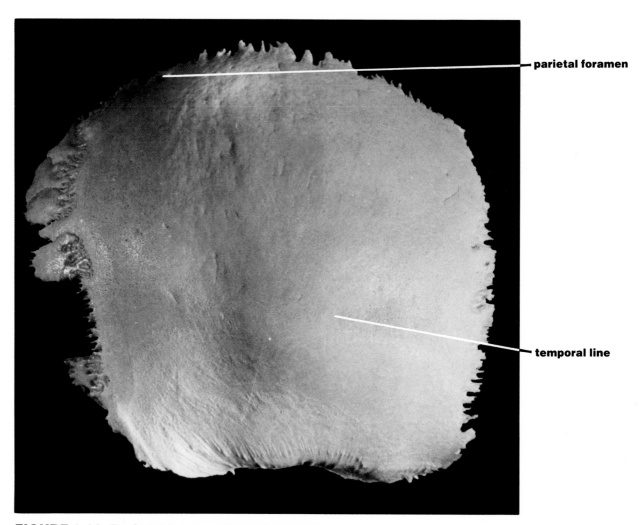

parietal foramen

temporal line

FIGURE 1-10. Parietal bone, external aspect.

INTRACRANIAL SURFACE (FIG. 1-11)

Sagittal Sulcus. Formed by both superior margins, and bisected by the sagittal suture, for the superior sagittal sinus.

Vessel Grooves. Very evident to seat the anterior and posterior middle meningeal vessels.

The four named bones articulating with the parietal bone are the **frontal** (one), **occipital** (one), **temporal** (two), and **sphenoid** (one).

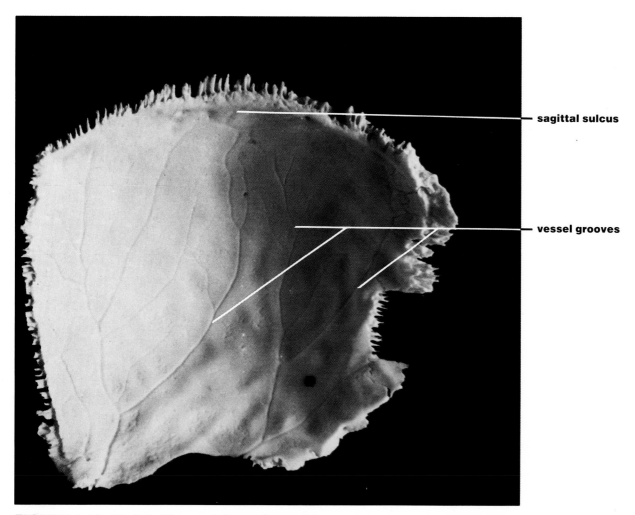

— sagittal sulcus

— vessel grooves

FIGURE 1-11. Parietal bone, internal aspect.

Occipital Bone (Figs. 1-12 and 1-13)

The occipital bone forms the posterior wall and a posterior wedge-shaped section of the cranial vault floor.

EXTERNAL SURFACE (FIG. 1-12)

Squama. Extending from the foramen magnum superior to the lambdoidal suture.

External Occipital Protuberance. A slight elevation in the median line approximately 4.5 cm superior to the foramen magnum.

Superior Nuchal Lines. Extending laterally from the external occipital protuberance (EOP).

Median Nuchal Line. Extending inferiorly from the EOP to the foramen magnum.

Inferior Nuchal Lines. Extending laterally from mid-median nuchal lines.

Basilar Part. Extending anterosuperiorly from the foramen magnum to articulate with the posterior surface of the sphenoid body.

Foramen Magnum. The large opening between the squama and the basilar part that transmits the medulla oblongata of the brain.

Occipital Condyles. Large, inferior swellings on each side of the foramen magnum for articulation with the lateral masses of the atlas.

Condyloid Canals. A small opening at the posterior base of each occipital condyle.

Hypoglossal Canals. Small openings anterior and superior to occipital condyles.

Jugular Process. Lateral to each occipital condyle, forming the posterior borders of the jugular foramina.

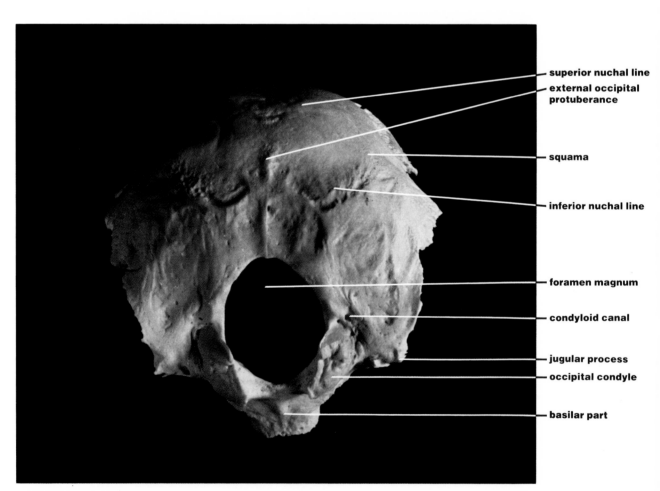

superior nuchal line
external occipital protuberance
squama
inferior nuchal line
foramen magnum
condyloid canal
jugular process
occipital condyle
basilar part

FIGURE 1-12. Occipital bone, external aspect.

INTRACRANIAL SURFACE (FIG. 1-13)

Fossae. Four separate fossae, two superior and two inferior, that make up the major portion of the internal squama.

Internal Occipital Protuberance. Elevated center point of the cruciate eminence that divides the four fossae.

Transverse Grooves. Extend laterally from either side of the internal occipital protuberance (IOP), separating the superior from the inferior fossae.

Internal Occipital Crest. Extends inferiorly from the IOP to the foramen magnum, separating the inferior fossae.

Jugular Notch. Extends anterolaterally from either side of the foramen magnum, forming the posterior margins of the jugular foramina.

The four named bones that articulate with the occipital are three cranial bones, the **parietal** (two), **temporal** (two), and **sphenoid** (one); and one cervical bone, the **atlas.**

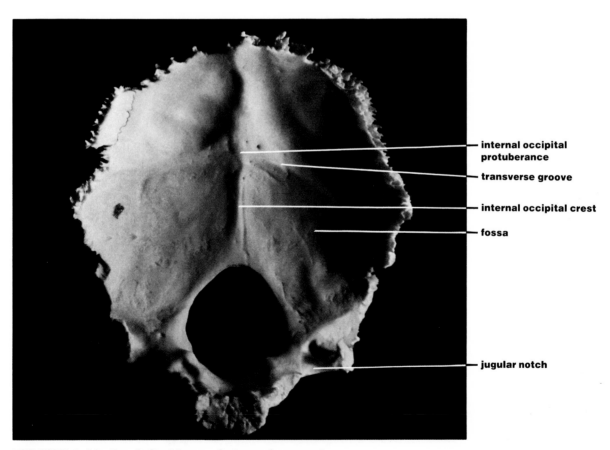

— internal occipital protuberance

— transverse groove

— internal occipital crest

— fossa

— jugular notch

FIGURE 1-13. Occipital bone, internal aspect.

Temporal Bone (Figs. 1-14 to 1-17)

A complex bone forming a portion of the lateral wall and mid-floor of the cranial vault, the temporal bone is generally classified into three major sections: squama, tympanic, and petrous.

SQUAMA

EXTERNAL SURFACE (FIG. 1-14). Slightly convex, the squama extends superiorly to articulate with the parietal bone and anteriorly to articulate with the great wing of the sphenoid.

Zygomatic process: Forming the posterior section of the zygomatic arch, the process extends anteriorly from the squama base to articulate with the temporal process of the zygomatic bone. The long axis of the arch is generally in line with the infraorbital meatal guideline.

Mandibular fossa: The mandibular fossa is a depression at the base (inferior surface) of the zygomatic process for receiving the condyle of the mandible. Its lateral, topographic location is approximately 2 cm anterior to the external auditory meatus.

Mastoid process: Associated with the squama as well as the petrous portion, the mastoid process is a rough, triangular-shaped bone posterior to the external auditory meatus. Its posterior border joins the occipital bone to form the occipitomastoid suture. The mastoid notch is found on its inferior surface, medial to the mastoid tip. As a reference for palpation, the inferior tip of the mastoid process is directly in line with the transverse process of the atlas. A large section of the mastoid process contains air cells. Located within the superoanterior part is a larger cavity, the tympanic antrum. The attic, or tympanic recess, is situated just anterior to the antrum.

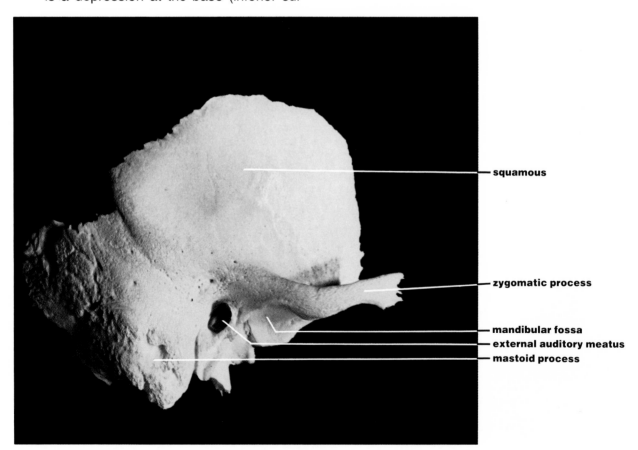

squamous

zygomatic process

mandibular fossa
external auditory meatus
mastoid process

FIGURE 1-14. Temporal bone, external aspect.

INTERNAL SURFACE (FIG. 1-15) The internal surface presents grooves, or sulci, for seating the middle meningeal vessels that are transmitted through the **foramen spinosum** of the sphenoid bone.

TYMPANIC

EXTERNAL SURFACE. The external surface provides a thin sheath of bone for the external auditory meatus, forming its anterior and lower posterior walls and floor.
External auditory meatus: The external auditory meatus is a short medial passageway whose roof and upper posterior wall, formed by the squama, is directed approximately 15 degrees superiorly and 15 degrees anteriorly, then ends internally at the tympanic membrane.
Styloid process: Directly anterior to the **mastoid notch,** on the inferior tympanic surface, the narrow, pointed styloid process extends inferiorly and slightly anteromedially.

INTERNAL SURFACE. The petrous portion becomes contiguous with the tympanic bone, about 2 cm medial to the outer surface of the external meatus.

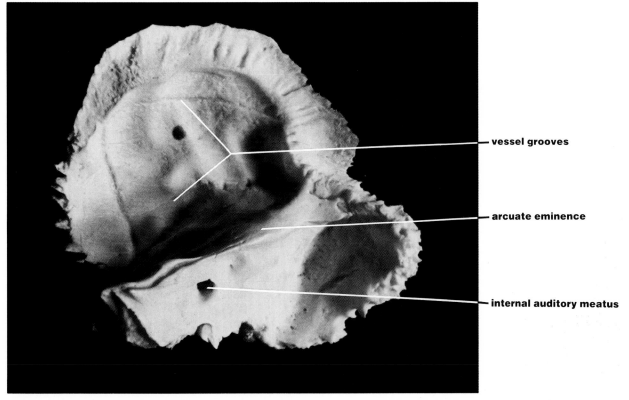

vessel grooves

arcuate eminence

internal auditory meatus

FIGURE 1-15. Temporal bone, medial aspect.

PETROUS (FIG. 1-16)

This portion, the most sophisticated, is also the most important radiographically. Generally classified as having a base (externally), an apex (medially), three surfaces, and a superior ridge, the long axis of the medial projection lies approximately 45 to 47 degrees between the coronal plane and the posterior sagittal plane in the mesocephalic skull.

Primary functions include housing the vestibulocochlear organ (inner ear) and the carotid canal.

BASE. The mastoid process and squama participate internally with the petrous portion to form the base.

APEX. The most medial-anterior projection of the petrous is generally serrated and articulates with the basion of the occipital bone. The inferomedial aspect of the apex provides a **carotid canal** for the internal carotid artery, and its posterolateral border participates with the sphenoid and occipital bones in the formation of the **foramen lacerum** as an upper exit for the same artery.

POSTERIOR SURFACE. Projecting inferiorly at a very steep incline, this surface forms the anterior wall of the posterior cranial fossa. Directly inferior and lateral to the posterior surface is a large deep groove, the **sigmoid sinus.** Directly superior to the **jugular foramen,** in the center medial surface, is the **internal acoustic meatus.**

ANTERIOR SURFACE. This gradual antero-inferior slope serves as the posterior partition for the medial cranial fossa.

INFERIOR SURFACE. This structure presents a very irregular surface (see Fig. 1-3). Of radiographic importance is a large round opening, midline of the petrous and approximately 2 cm lateral to the apex, called the carotid foramen or opening into the carotid canal. Directly posterior to this opening is a deep depression, called the jugular fossa, that houses the internal jugular vein.

SUPERIOR (PETROUS) RIDGE. The **arcuate eminence,** which is formed from the anterior surface, appears radiographically as the highest point of the petrous ridge. It is important for locating the superior semicircular canal, and subsequently is the landmark for locating the internal ear.

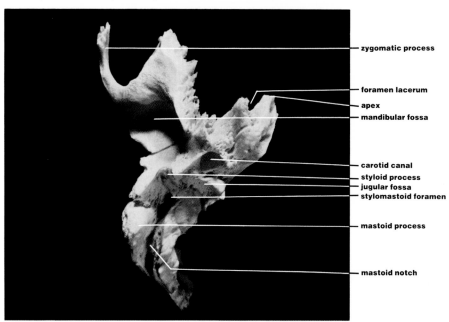

— zygomatic process

— foramen lacerum
— apex
— mandibular fossa

— carotid canal
— styloid process
— jugular fossa
— stylomastoid foramen

— mastoid process

— mastoid notch

FIGURE 1-16. Temporal bone, inferior aspect.

MIDDLE EAR (FIG. 1-17). Directly inferior to the **arcuate eminence** and within the temporal bone is the tympanic cavity. As the cavity is approached from the external acoustic meatus, the first structure contacted is the tympanic membrane. Adjacent to the medial surface of the membrane is the first auditory ossicle, the **malleus,** whose globular head extends up into the **attic,** or **epitympanic recess,** which is superior to the tympanic membrane. The second ossicle, the **incus,** joins the malleus at its head and connects with the third ossicle, the **stapes,** by way of the lenticular process. The base of this "stirrup-shaped" bone connects with the margin of the fenestra vestibuli of the internal ear or labyrinth.

LABYRINTH. This most important component of the acoustic system is located medial and adjacent to the middle ear to receive the base of the stapes. The name labyrinth is appropriate in that the structure consists of a series of canals hollowed out within the petrous region and classified into three sections: the **vestibule, cochlea,** and **semicircular canals.**

Vestibule: As the mid-body of the labyrinth, its lateral wall contains the fenestra vestibuli that receives the base of the stapes. The five openings for the semicircular canals are found in the posterior section. The posterior and superior semicircular canals share a common opening, whereas the lateral canal uses two openings. Concurrent with the anterior wall is the cochlea.

Cochlea: The internal spiral canal of the cone-shaped cochlea provides for one opening each into the tympanic cavity, the vestibule, and inferior surface of the petrous portion.

Semicircular canals: The superior, lateral, and posterior canals open into the posterior section of the vestibule by five openings, three of which are larger ampullas. The superior canal is located directly under the arcuate eminence and presents an inverted V pattern on special anteroposterior and posteroanterior projections of the petrous portion. The semicircular canals, cochlea, and middle ear components help make up the "star pattern" seen on radiographs, which results from the abovementioned projections.

The five named bones articulating with the temporal are three cranial bones, the **sphenoid** (one), **parietal** (two), and **occipital** (one); and two facial bones, the **zygomatic** (two) and the **mandible** (one).

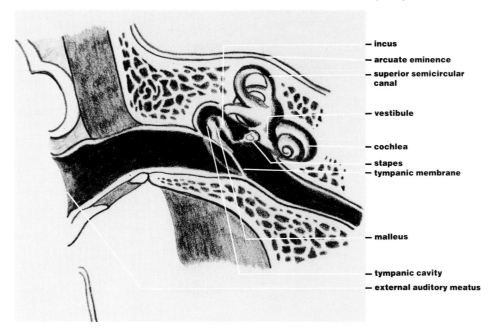

- incus
- arcuate eminence
- superior semicircular canal
- vestibule
- cochlea
- stapes
- tympanic membrane
- malleus
- tympanic cavity
- external auditory meatus

FIGURE 1-17. Temporal bone, section through mid-petrous portion.

Sphenoid Bone (Figs. 1-18 and 1-19)

Commonly termed the "bat-wing" bone, the sphenoid is situated in the mid-cranial floor, with large wing-like appendages extended anterolaterally and smaller processes extended inferiorly.

The body, situated in the midline of the cranial floor, houses the sphenoidal sinus.

ANTERIOR ASPECT

Extending from the midline of the body, the sphenoidal crest joins with the perpendicular plate of the ethmoid to help form the posterosuperior section of the nasal septum. Laterally, the greater wings provide the posterior walls of the orbital cavities. The posterior walls of the nasal cavity are also formed by the anterior surface of the sphenoid body.

The anterior pterygoid margins articulate anteriorly with the palatine bones.

SUPERIOR ASPECT

LESSER WINGS. Anterior and superior to the body, these thin, shelf-like bones terminate laterally as very fine projections. Each wing articulates anteriorly with frontal bone to help form the orbital roof. The superior orbital fissure is formed by the inferior border. **Optic foramina,** for transmission of the optic nerve, are situated within the **lesser wing,** with the long axis of the optic canals approximately 40 degrees from the median plane. Posterior projections form the **anterior clinoid processes.**

BODY. Anterior, between the optic foramina, is the **chiasmatic groove** that seats the optic chiasma. Slightly posterior is the **tuberculum sellae;** located between the middle clinoid processes, it forms the anterior wall of the **hypophyseal fossa (sella turcica),** which seats the pitu-

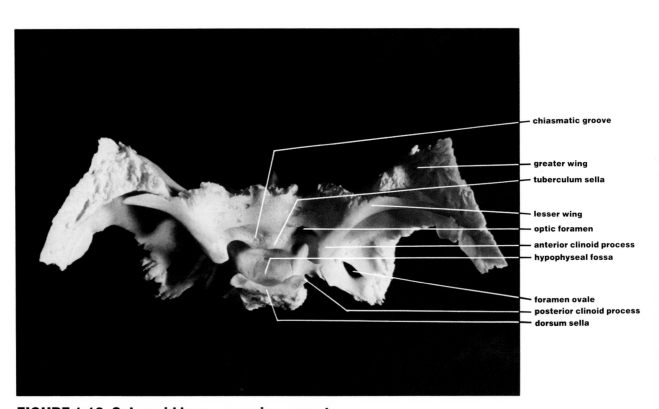

— chiasmatic groove

— greater wing
— tuberculum sella

— lesser wing
— optic foramen
— anterior clinoid process
— hypophyseal fossa

— foramen ovale
— posterior clinoid process
— dorsum sella

FIGURE 1-18. Sphenoid bone, superior aspect.

itary gland. The posterior wall is formed by the **dorsum sellae,** which terminates on each side as the **posterior clinoid processes.** Occasionally, radiographic studies will demonstrate the anterior and posterior clinoids fused together. The clivus extends posteroinferiorly from the dorsum sellae to articulate with the basilar part of the occipital bone.

GREATER WINGS.
Extending both anteriorly and laterally from the body, the greater wings form the posterior walls of the orbital cavities and the anterior walls of the middle cranial fossae. The superior borders complete the formation of superior orbital fissures with the lesser wings. Directly beneath the orbital fissure, and in a posterolateral line, are three foramina: the **foramen rotundum, foramen ovale,** and the smaller **foramen spinosum.**

POSTERIOR ASPECT

ROSTRUM.
This pointed process extends inferiorly from the body to articulate with the vomer and continues anteriorly to become continuous with the sphenoidal crest.

PTERYGOID PROCESSES.
Extending inferiorly from the union of the body and greater wings, each pterygoid process demonstrates a **lateral** and a **medial plate,** forming the deep **pterygoid fossa.** Each medial plate terminates inferiorly into a fragile **hamulus process.**

The eight named bones articulating with the sphenoid are five cranial bones, the **frontal** (one), **parietal** (two), **occipital** (one), **temporal** (two), and **ethmoid** (one); and three facial bones, the **vomer** (one), **zygomatic** (two), and **palatine** (two).

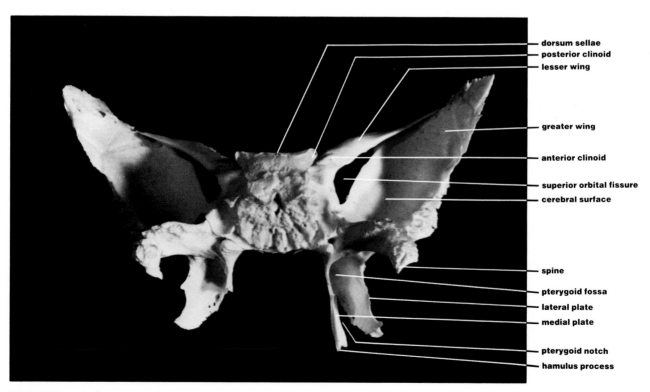

dorsum sellae
posterior clinoid
lesser wing

greater wing

anterior clinoid

superior orbital fissure
cerebral surface

spine

pterygoid fossa
lateral plate
medial plate

pterygoid notch
hamulus process

FIGURE 1-19. Sphenoid bone, posterior aspect.

Ethmoid Bone (Figs. 1-20 and 1-21)

The ethmoid is a very fragile bone situated anterior to the sphenoid and superiorly within the nasal cavity between the orbital cavities.

ANTERIOR ASPECT

Radiographically demonstrated within the nasal cavity is a thin medial partition, the perpendicular plate, that articulates with the sphenoid, frontal, nasal, and vomer to help form part of the nasal septum. In line with the **perpendicular plate,** projected superiorly above the level of a horizontal plate, is a pointed process, the **crista galli (cock's comb),** for the attachment of the falx cerebri. Immediately lateral to either side of the plate, extending downward, are the middle nasal concha (turbinate) bones.

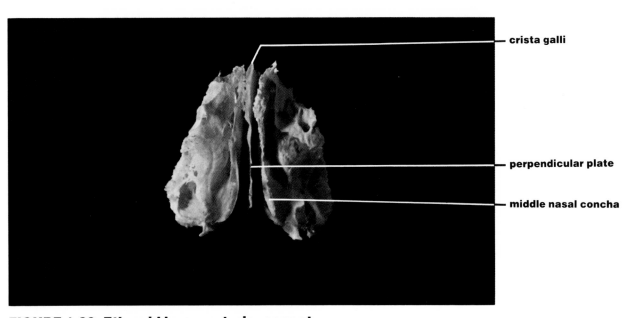

crista galli

perpendicular plate

middle nasal concha

FIGURE 1-20. Ethmoid bone, anterior aspect.

SUPERIOR ASPECT

Horizontally within a deep groove on either side of the crista galli is the **cribriform plate,** which is perforated with many small holes to transmit olfactory nerve fibers.

Within the lateral masses, on either side of the perpendicular plate, are numerous, thin-walled cavities called the ethmoidal sinuses.

The eight named bones articulating with the ethmoid are two cranial bones, the **sphenoid** (one) and the **frontal** (one); and six facial bones, the **palatine** (two), **vomer** (one), **inferior nasal conchae** (two), **maxillae** (two), **lacrimals** (two), and **nasal** (two).

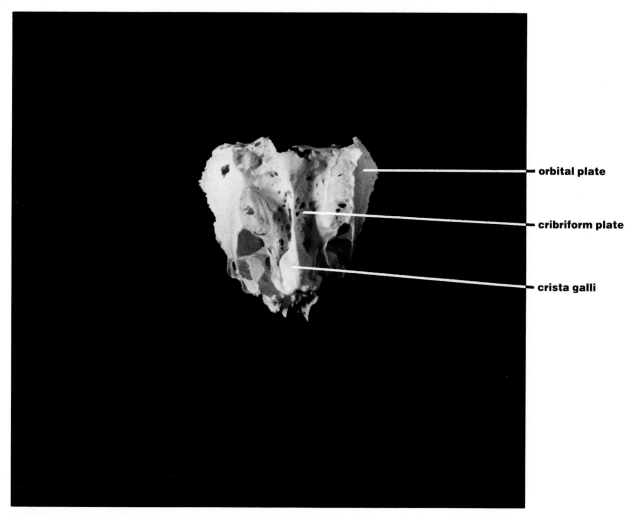

orbital plate

cribriform plate

crista galli

FIGURE 1-21. Ethmoid bone, superior aspect.

FACIAL BONES

Palatine Bones (Fig. 1-22)

Each palatine bone is a thin, L-shaped bone situated in the posterolateral and inferior sections of the nasal cavity.

VERTICAL PORTION. The vertical portion of the palatine bone provides for the posterolateral wall of the nasal cavity and a small concave surface (orbital) on the superior aspect for participating in the floor of the orbital cavity. The lateral border contributes in the posterior design of the inferior orbital fissure.

The medial wall provides for the attachment of the inferior nasal concha bone.

HORIZONTAL PORTION (PLATE). The horizontal portion provides for the posterior floor of the nasal cavity as well as the posterior quarter of the hard palate. It articulates with palatine process of the maxillary along its anterior border by way of the transverse palatine suture.

The six named bones articulating with the palatine are two cranial bones, the **ethmoid** (one) and **sphenoid** (one); and four facial bones, the adjacent **palatine** (two), **vomer** (one), **inferior nasal concha** (two), and **maxilla** (two).

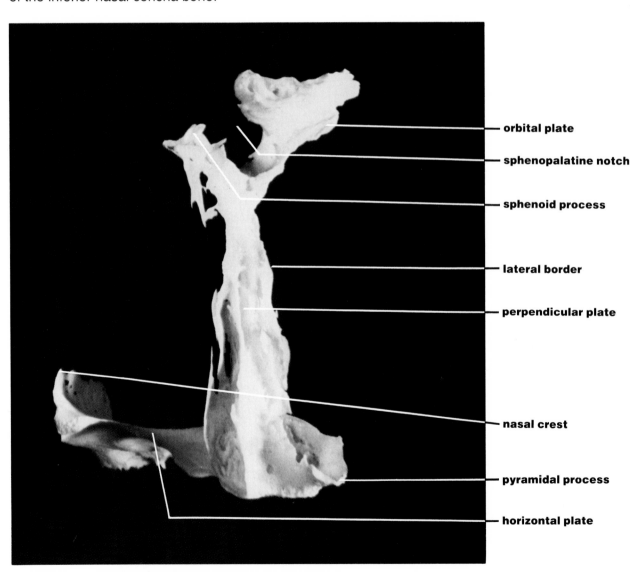

— orbital plate

— sphenopalatine notch

— sphenoid process

— lateral border

— perpendicular plate

— nasal crest

— pyramidal process

— horizontal plate

FIGURE 1-22. Palatine bone, posterior aspect.

Vomer Bone (Fig. 1-23)

The vomer is a thin blade-like bone whose **base** (ala) articulates with the medial-inferior surface of the sphenoidal body, then extends inferiorly and anteriorly to participate in the composition of the nasal septum.

The four named bones articulating with the vomer are two cranial bones, the **ethmoid** (one) and **sphenoid** (one); and two facial bones, the **palatine** (two) and the **maxilla** (two).

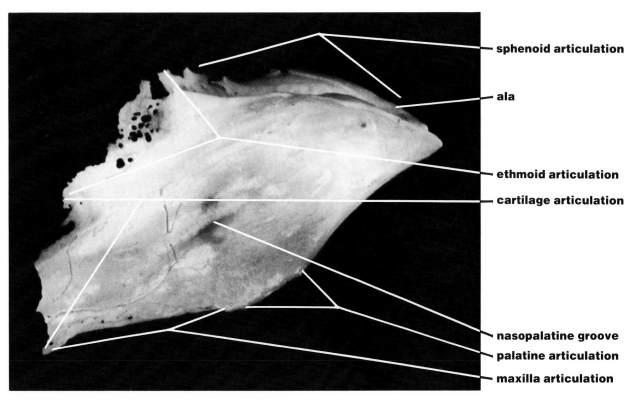

FIGURE 1-23. Vomer bone, lateral aspect.

- sphenoid articulation
- ala
- ethmoid articulation
- cartilage articulation
- nasopalatine groove
- palatine articulation
- maxilla articulation

Inferior Nasal Concha Bones (Figs. 1-24 and 1-25)

This thin, delicate bone is attached to the lateral wall of the nasal cavity. Approximately 3 cm horizontally, the thin plate extends inferiorly, then curls up laterally.

The four named bones articulating with the inferior nasal concha are one cranial bone, the **ethmoid** (one); and three facial bones, the **palatine** (two), **maxillary** (two), and **lacrimal** (two).

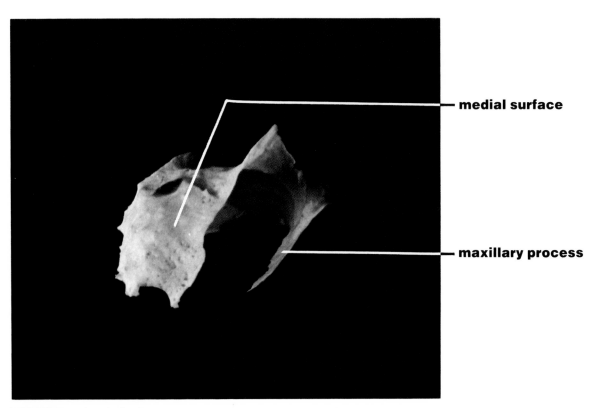

medial surface

maxillary process

FIGURE 1-24. Inferior nasal concha bone, anterior aspect.

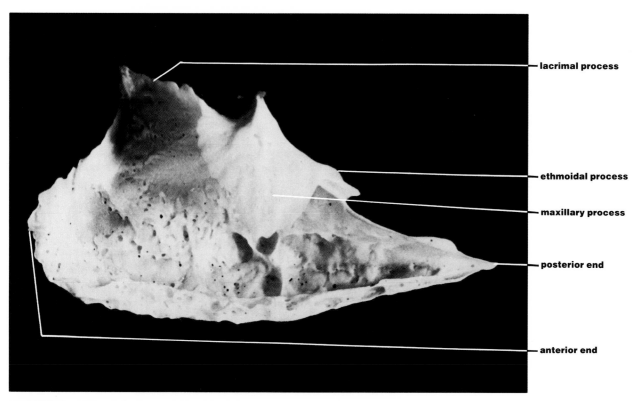

lacrimal process

ethmoidal process

maxillary process

posterior end

anterior end

FIGURE 1-25. Inferior nasal concha bone, lateral aspect.

Maxillary Bones (Figs. 1-26 and 1-27)

These large bones of the mid-facial region join to form the upper jaw. Four major processes encompass the centralized body of each maxillary bone.

BODY. The walls of the body, along with the roof and floor, encapsulate the large **maxillary sinus (antrum of Highmore).** The anterior surface displays the **infraorbital foramen** beneath the midorbital margin. The **anterior nasal spine (acanthion process)** is formed at the anteroinferior border of the nasal cavity. The medial wall assists in the composition of the lateral wall of the nasal cavity and for the attachment of the inferior nasal concha bone. The roof participates in a large section of the orbital cavity floor and joins the posterior wall in forming the posteroinferior margin of the inferior orbital fissure.

FRONTAL PROCESS. The frontal process extends medially and superiorly to articulate with the frontal bone while forming the medial margin of the orbital cavity. It participates with the lacrimal bone in forming the **lacrimal fossa.**

PALATINE PROCESS. The palatine process joins the adjacent palatine process at the median palatine suture to form the majority of the hard palate and subsequently the anterior floor of the nasal cavity. At the anteromedial junction of the hard palate is the **incisive foramen.**

ALVEOLAR PROCESS. The inferior ridge around the anterolateral border of the hard palate provides special gomphotic articulations for housing the teeth roots of two incisors, one canine, two premolars, and three molars for each maxillary bone.

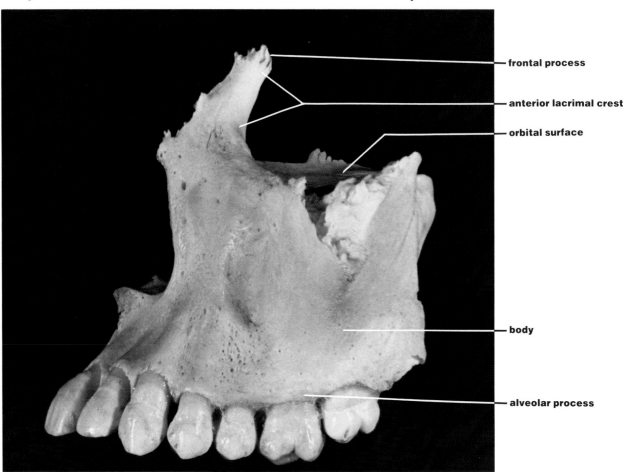

frontal process

anterior lacrimal crest

orbital surface

body

alveolar process

FIGURE 1-26. Maxillary bone, lateral aspect.

ZYGOMATIC PROCESS. The zygomatic process extends laterally to join the zygomatic bone in forming the prominent portion of the cheek and the **infratemporal fossa.**

The nine named bones that articulate with the maxillary are two cranial bones, the **ethmoid** (one) and **frontal** (one); and seven facial bones, the adjacent **maxillary** (two), **inferior nasal concha** (two), **lacrimal** (two), **nasal** (two), **zygomatic** (two), **vomer** (one), and **palatine** (two).

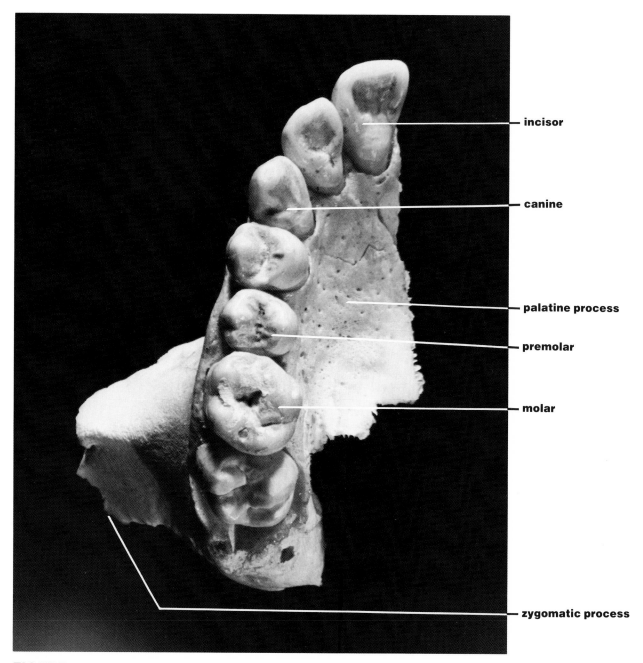

— incisor

— canine

— palatine process

— premolar

— molar

— zygomatic process

FIGURE 1-27. Maxillary bone, inferior aspect.

Nasal Bones (Fig. 1-28)

From their articulation with the frontal bone, the two thin nasal bones slope downward to form the "bridge" of the nose. From their union at the intranasal suture, a small crest extends inward to participate in the design of the nasal septum.

The four named bones that articulate with the nasal are two cranial bones, the **frontal** (one) and the **ethmoid** (one); and two facial bones, the adjacent **nasal** (two) and the **maxilla** (two).

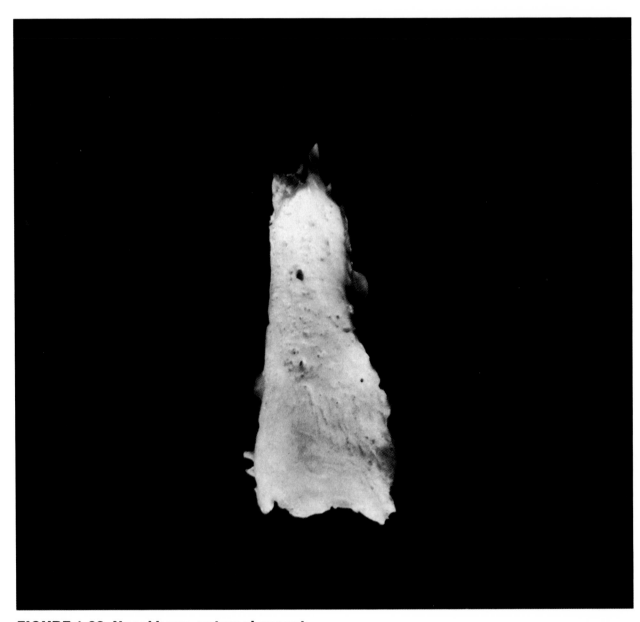

FIGURE 1-28. Nasal bone, external aspect.

Lacrimal Bones (Fig. 1-29)

The very tiny, shell-like lacrimal participates with the maxillary in forming the posterior portion of the **lacrimal fossa.** The lacrimal bone is located just anterior to the ethmoid and posterior to the frontal process of the maxillary, inside the medial wall of the orbital cavity. Inside the lacrimal fossa is the lacrimal groove for seating the nasolacrimal duct.

The four named bones that articulate with the lacrimal are two cranial bones, the **ethmoid** (one) and **frontal** (one); and two facial bones, the **zygomatic** (two) and **maxillary** (two).

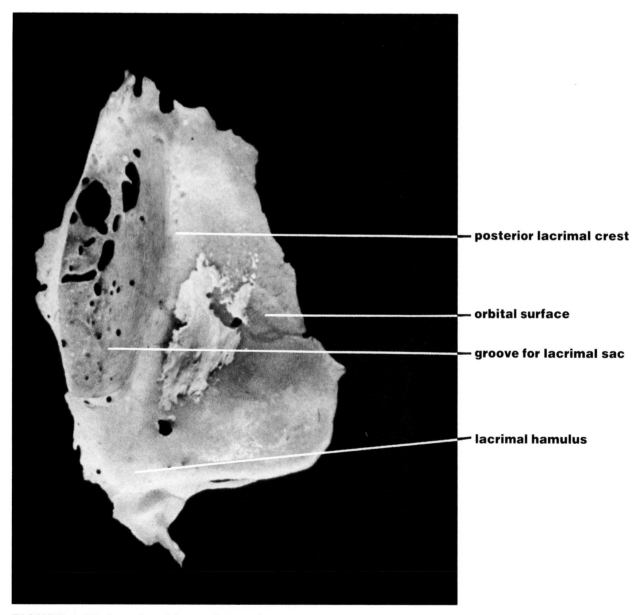

posterior lacrimal crest

orbital surface

groove for lacrimal sac

lacrimal hamulus

FIGURE 1-29. Lacrimal bone, lateral aspect.

Zygomatic Bones (Fig. 1-30)

Shaped somewhat like an arrowhead with its three major processes, the zygoma is sometimes referred to as the malar, or cheek, bone.

ORBITAL SURFACE. The orbital surface forms the lateral wall and the inferolateral ridge of the bony orbital margin.

MAXILLARY PROCESS. The maxillary process articulates with the lateral, zygomatic process of the maxillary bone.

FRONTAL PROCESS. The frontal process projects superiorly to join the zygomatic process of the frontal bone.

TEMPORAL PROCESS. The temporal process extends posteriorly to unite with the zygomatic process of the temporal bone in the formation of zygomatic arch. The long axis of the zygomatic arch is generally in line with the infraorbitomeatal guideline.

The four named bones that articulate with the zygomatic bone are three cranial bones, the **sphenoid** (one), **frontal** (one), and **temporal** (two); and one facial bone, the **maxillary** (two).

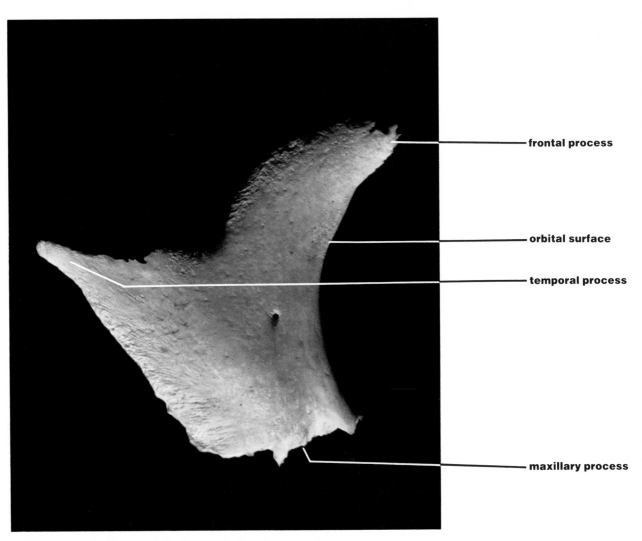

FIGURE 1-30. Zygomatic bone, lateral aspect.

Mandible Bone(s) (Figs. 1-31 to 1-33)

The largest of the facial bones, the two lateral sections of the mandible fuse in early life at the **mandibular symphysis (symphysis menti)** to form the lower jaw.

ANTERIOR SURFACE. The anterior surface presents a portion of the **alveolar process** with two **central** and two **lateral incisor teeth,** and one **canine tooth** on each side of the four incisors.

Symphysis Menti. The symphysis menti is the vertical union of the lateral portions, forming a slight ridge.

Mental Protuberance. The mental protuberance is a raised area at the inferior end of the symphysis menti.

LATERAL SURFACE. The lateral surface presents two flat areas: one vertical, the ramus; one horizontal, the body.

Body. The body extends from the anterior symphysis menti, posterior to the anterior, oblique line of the **ramus,** which is a slightly inferior, sloping ridge in line with the second and third molars.
Mental foramen: This small external foramen, in line with the second premolar, transmits the mental vessels and nerve.

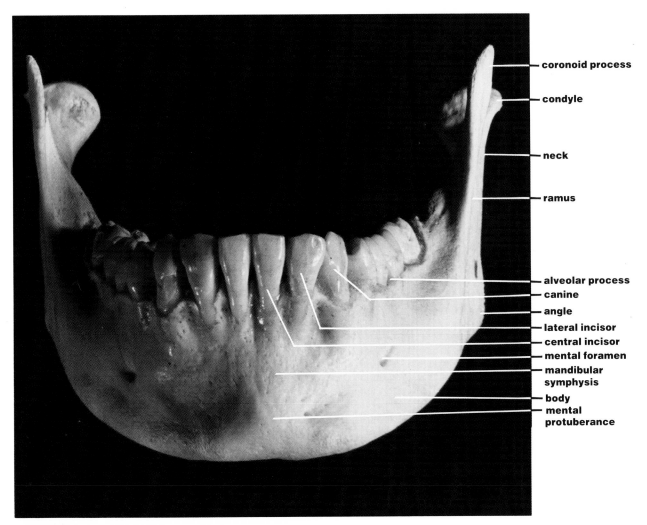

FIGURE 1-31. Mandible, anterior aspect.

coronoid process
condyle
neck
ramus
alveolar process
canine
angle
lateral incisor
central incisor
mental foramen
mandibular symphysis
body
mental protuberance

Ramus. This flat vertical portion extends vertically from the oblique line to the tip of the condyle.

Angle: This is a curved area at posteroinferior border.

Coronoid process: The coronoid process is a round process at the anterosuperior aspect for the attachment of the buccinator and temporalis muscles.

Condyle: The condyle is a round, smooth swelling at the posterosuperior aspect for articulation with the condylar fossa of the temporal bone.

Neck: The neck is inferior to the condyle.

Mandibular notch: Sometimes referred to as the semilunar notch, the curved depression is situated between the coronoid process and the condyle.

MEDIAL SURFACE. One foramen, the **mandibular,** is located in the center of the vertical ramus for transmitting the inferior alveolar vessels and nerve.

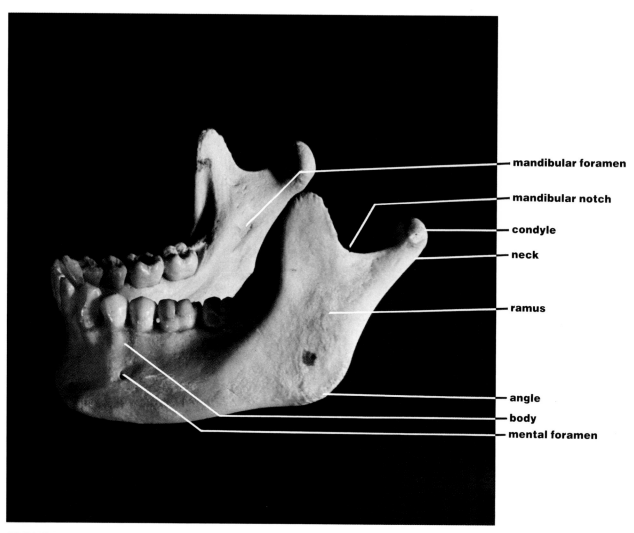

FIGURE 1-32. Mandible, lateral aspect.

SUPERIOR SURFACE. The alveolar ridge provides special gomphotic articulations for two incisors, one canine, two premolars, and three molars on each side.

The one named cranial bone that articulates with the mandible is the **temporal** (two).

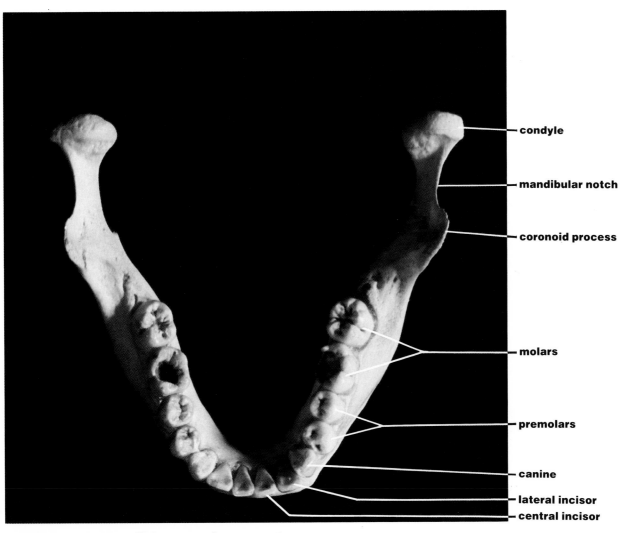

FIGURE 1-33. Mandible, superior aspect.

condyle
mandibular notch
coronoid process
molars
premolars
canine
lateral incisor
central incisor

SELECTED FORAMINA

Basal Foramina (Figs. 1-34 and 1-35)

CAROTID ORIFICE (TWO). The carotid orifice is an opening into the carotid canal that is situated on the inferomedial surface of the petrous portion of the temporal bone for passage of the internal carotid artery.

HYPOGLOSSAL CANAL (TWO). The hypoglossal canal is situated superior to the midbase of the occipital condyle. This structure is for passage of a pharyngeal artery branch and the hypoglossal nerve.

INTERNAL AUDITORY FORAMEN (TWO). This is a medium-sized opening situated on the posterior wall of the petrous portion, forming the entrance of the internal auditory meatus. It is for passage of auditory and facial nerves.

JUGULAR FORAMEN (TWO). A large irregular opening between the posteroinferior border of the petrous portion and the occipital bone, the jugular foramen is for passage of the internal jugular vein and the vagus and glossopharyngeal nerves.

FORAMEN LACERUM (TWO). A large irregular opening at the anteromedial end of the petrous apex, the foramen lacerum is formed by the temporal, sphenoid, and occipital bones. The internal carotid artery enters the skull after exiting through the foramen.

FORAMEN MAGNUM (ONE). The foramen magnum is a very large opening in the basal part of the occipital bone through which the medulla oblongata of the brain passes.

FORAMEN OVALE (TWO). The foramen ovale is an oblong opening in the posteroinferior margin of the great wing of the sphenoid bone for passage of the mandibular branch of the trigeminal (fifth cranial) nerve.

FORAMEN ROTUNDUM (TWO). The foramen rotundum is a small opening directly between the junction of the superior and inferior orbital fissures on either side of the sphenoidal body for passage of the maxillary division of the trigeminal (fifth cranial) nerve.

FORAMEN SPINOSUM (TWO). The foramen spinosum is a very small opening posterolateral and adjacent to the foramen ovale in the posterior margin of the great wing of the sphenoid bone for passage of the middle meningeal artery to the cranial artery.

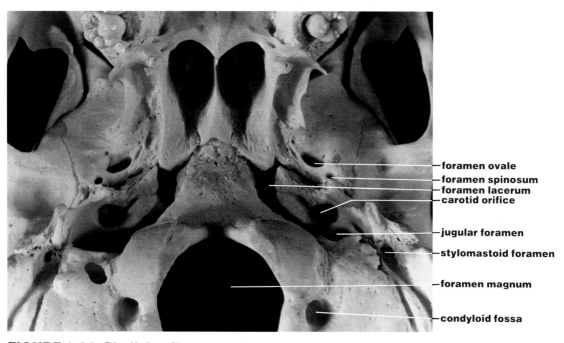

- foramen ovale
- foramen spinosum
- foramen lacerum
- carotid orifice
- jugular foramen
- stylomastoid foramen
- foramen magnum
- condyloid fossa

FIGURE 1-34. Skull, basilar aspect.

Frontal Bone

SUPRAORBITAL NOTCH (TWO). The supraorbital notch is a very small depression in the superomedial margin of the orbital cavity. It houses the supraorbital nerve and vessel (see Fig. 1-1).

Mandible

MANDIBULAR FORAMEN (TWO). The mandibular foramen is an opening, projecting inferiorly, on the medial side of the ramus for passage of the mandibular nerve. A nerve branch supplies each lower tooth (see Fig. 1-32).

MENTAL FORAMEN (TWO). The mental foramen is a small opening in the lateral body, below and in line with the second premolar, for passage of the mandibular nerve (see Fig. 1-1).

Maxilla

INCISIVE FORAMEN (ONE). The incisive foramen is formed by the two palatine processes of the maxilla and located in the anterior midline of the hard palate for passage of the nasopalatine nerve and palatine artery (see Fig. 1-3).

INFRAORBITAL FORAMEN (TWO). The infraorbital foramen is situated directly beneath the midinfraorbital margin for passage of the infraorbital nerve and artery (see Fig. 1-1).

Orbital Cavity

OPTIC FORAMEN (TWO). Situated within the lesser wing of the sphenoid and located in the posteromedial apex of the cavity, the optic foramen is for passage of the optic nerve and the ophthalmic artery (see Fig. 1-1).

INFERIOR ORBITAL FISSURE (TWO). This fissure is formed by the greater wing of the sphenoid, maxillary, palatine, and zygomatic bones and is located in the posteroinferior floor of the cavity. It is for passage of the maxillary nerve branches and the infraorbital vessels (see Fig. 1-1).

SUPERIOR ORBITAL FISSURE (TWO). The superior orbital fissure is formed by the lesser and greater wings of the sphenoid, by the body of the sphenoid medially, and by the orbital plate of the frontal bone laterally. It is for passage of the trigeminal nerve branches, middle meningeal artery, superior ophthalmic vein, and lacrimal artery branch (see Fig. 1-1).

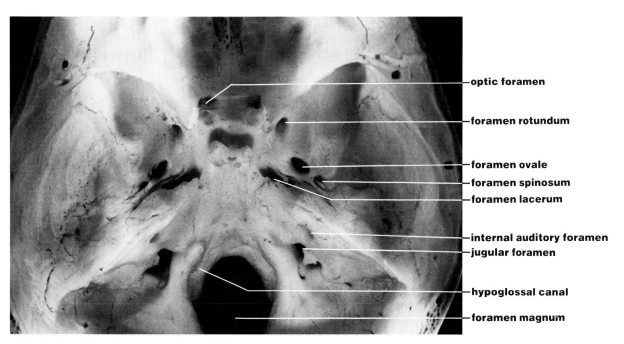

— optic foramen
— foramen rotundum
— foramen ovale
— foramen spinosum
— foramen lacerum
— internal auditory foramen
— jugular foramen
— hypoglossal canal
— foramen magnum

FIGURE 1-35. Skull, cranial aspect.

BIBLIOGRAPHY

DULAC, GL, CLAUS, E, AND BARROIS, J: *Oto-Radiology.* In *X-Ray Bulletin,* special ed. AGFA-Gevaert, Antwerp, 1973.

GOSS, CM: *Gray's Anatomy,* ed 29. Lea & Febiger, Philadelphia, 1975.

JACOBI, CA AND PARIS, DQ: *Textbook of Radiologic Technology,* ed 6. CV Mosby, St. Louis, 1977.

MERRILL, V: *Atlas of Roentgenographic Positions and Standard Radiologic Procedures, Vol 2,* ed 4. CV Mosby, St. Louis, 1975.

MESCHAN, I: *An Atlas of Anatomy Basic to Radiology.* WB Saunders, Philadelphia, 1975.

MONTGOMERY, RL: *Basic Anatomy for the Allied Health Professions.* Urban & Schwarzenberg, Baltimore, 1981.

THOMPSON, TT: *Primer of Clinical Radiology,* ed 2. Little, Brown & Co, Boston, 1980.

SKULL LOCALIZATIONS AND CLASSIFICATIONS

UNIT

2

PLANES AND MOVEMENTS

Of all the different parts of the human anatomy, the skull requires the most critical positioning accuracy owing to the many processes and foramina that are very intricate in design.

Although the majority of skulls are radiographically classified as average (mesocephalic) in size and shape, there are occasions when a variation from the average will require special rotations in skull positioning. The areas of the skull that are most affected by variations in skull conformations are the petrous regions. It is necessary, therefore, that all radiographers who desire to perfect the art of craniographic positioning implement craniographic measurements and cephalic indexing as integral parts of their routines.

In preparation for learning how to properly classify skulls for radiographic purposes, it is necessary to become familiar with the localizing planes and reference points that play an important part in each radiographic position.

Below are line drawings with appropriate localizing terms and definitions.

Planes of the Skull (Figs. 2-1 to 2-3)

MIDSAGITTAL OR MEDIAN. Separates the skull into right and left halves.

SAGITTAL. Separates the skull into right and left portions (unequal).

HORIZONTAL OR TRANSVERSE. Separates the skull into superior and inferior portions.

CORONAL. Separates the skull into anterior and posterior portions.

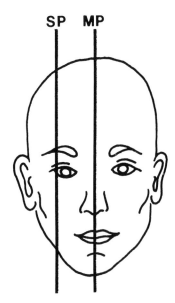

FIGURE 2-1. Anterior aspect with planes.

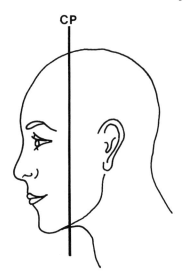

FIGURE 2-2. Anterior aspect with planes.

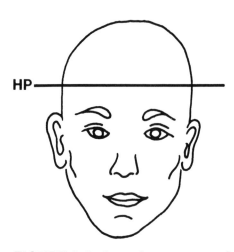

FIGURE 2-3. Lateral aspect with planes.

Movements of the Skull
(Figs. 2-4 to 2-8)

TILT RIGHT. Lateral bending at the neck, with the vertex toward the patient's right.

TILT LEFT. Lateral bending at the neck, with the vertex toward the patient's left.

FLEXION. Anterior or forward bending at the neck.

EXTENSION. Posterior or backward bending at the neck.

ROTATION. Turning around a central axis or pivot point.

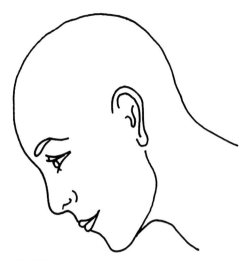

FIGURE 2-6. Lateral aspect, flexion.

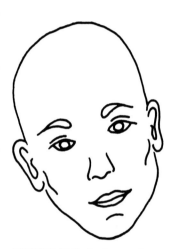

FIGURE 2-4. Anterior aspect, tilt right.

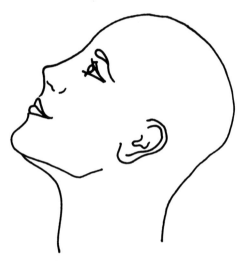

FIGURE 2-7. Lateral aspect, extension.

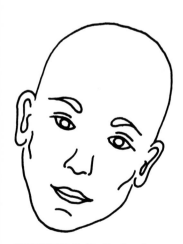

FIGURE 2-5. Anterior aspect, tilt left.

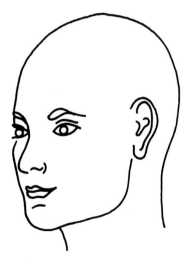

FIGURE 2-8. Anterior oblique aspect, rotation.

When critiquing radiographs, it should be noted that it is possible to incorporate flexion *OR* extension with any combination of tilt and rotation, thus causing multiple corrections to be considered. Figure 2-9 shows a radiograph of a true anterior view of the skull. Figure 2-10 shows a radiograph of an anterior view of the skull with increased extension, tilt, and increased rotation.

Throughout the positioning units of this textbook, you will find examples of how excessive head manipulations or tube angulations will affect the anatomic structures under consideration; these examples provide a guide for comparison study and effective learning as well as a "blueprint" of instruction for corrective measures.

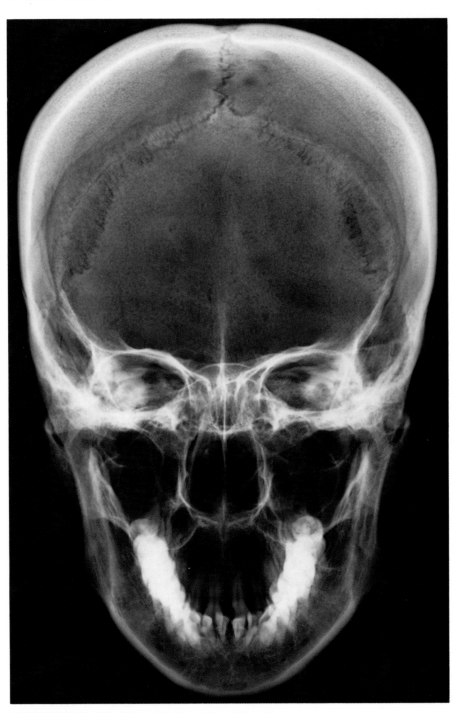

FIGURE 2-9. Skull, anterior view (true).

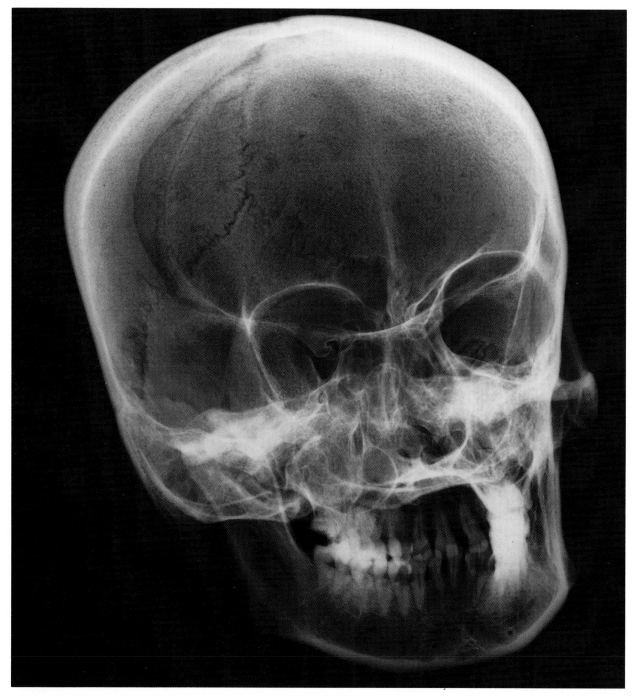

FIGURE 2-10. Skull, anterior view (extension, tilt, and rotation).

RADIOGRAPHIC LINES AND REFERENCE POINTS

Although some of the names of radiographic lines have changed over the years, this book will associate the names of lines with the current use of anatomic structures.

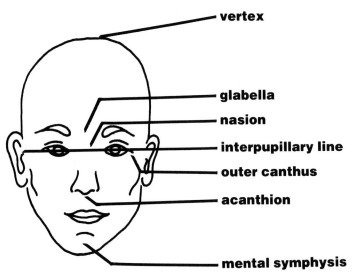

FIGURE 2-11. Anterior aspect with guidelines and reference points.

Radiographic Lines (Figs. 2-11 and 2-12)

ACANTHIOMEATAL LINE. A line connecting the anterior nasal spine and the external auditory meatus.

CANTHOMEATAL LINE (REID'S BASE LINE). A line connecting the outer canthus of the eye with the external auditory meatus.

GLABELLOALVEOLAR LINE. A line connecting the anterior surface of the glabella and the anterior alveolar process of the maxilla.

GLABELLOMEATAL LINE. A line connecting the center of the glabella with the external auditory meatus.

INFRAORBITOMEATAL LINE. A line connecting the inferior margin of the orbital cavity and the external auditory meatus.

INTERPUPILLARY LINE. A line connecting the pupils of eyes at the approximate level of the nasion.

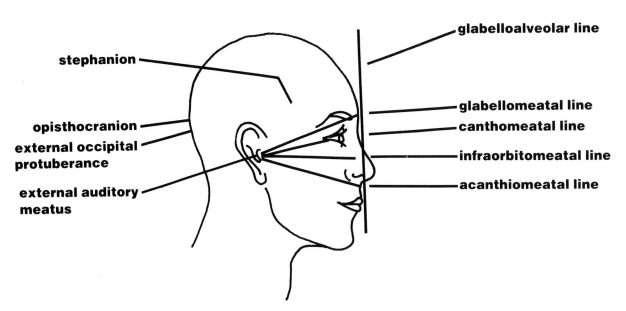

FIGURE 2-12. Lateral aspect with guidelines and reference points.

Reference Points
(Figs. 2-11 and 2-12)

ACANTHION. Tip of the anterior nasal spine.

EXTERNAL AUDITORY MEATUS (EAM). External opening and canal leading to the tympanic membrane.

EXTERNAL OCCIPITAL PROTUBERANCE (EOP). A swelling or raised area on the posteroinferior surface of the occipital bone in the medial plane.

GLABELLA. Center point between the superciliary arches on the anterior frontal area.

INION. Synonymous with external occipital protuberance.

MENTAL SYMPHYSIS. Anteroinferior point at the union of the mandibular bodies.

NASION. Depression at the junction of the nasal and frontal bones.

OPISTHOCRANION. Most posterior point on the external surface of the occipital bone.

OUTER CANTHUS. Lateral junction of the upper and lower eyelids.

STEPHANION. Junction where the superior temporal ridge crosses the coronal suture.

VERTEX. Uppermost point, or apex, of the cranial vault.

SKULL CLASSIFICATIONS

Cephalic Index
(Figs. 2-13 to 2-15)

Cephalic indexing is a term applied to the use of two basic measurements of the cranial vault to determine the ratio of the length to the breadth (width). The formula is: the breadth × 100 divided by the length.

BREADTH. Measured with centimeter calipers at the level of the stephanion, from skin surface to skin surface.

LENGTH. Measured with centimeter calipers from the center of the glabella to the opisthocranion point, from skin surface to skin surface.

There are three general classifications of adult skull sizes that will directly affect radiographic positioning accuracy, primarily in structures of the petrous portion of the temporal bone. The three classifications are:

MESOCEPHALIC. Average-sized skull, with a 45- to 47-degree measurement between the long axis of the petrous portion, on one side, and the posteromedian plane of the skull. The cephalic index ratio should fall between 76.0 and 80.9.

DOLICHOCEPHALIC. Narrow or elongated skull, with a 40-degree measurement between the long axis of the petrous portion, on one side, and the posteromedian plane of the skull. The cephalic index ratio should fall at 75.9 or below.

BRACHYCEPHALIC. Short, wide skull, with a 54-degree measurement between the long axis of the petrous portion, on one side, and the posteromedian plane of the skull. The cephalic index ratio should fall at 81.0 or above.

For example, from a true supine position, in order to determine the amount of head rotation needed in a patient when it is necessary to place the long axis of the petrous portion on the right side parallel to the surface of the film holder, you must first classify the skull size by ce-phalic indexing, then rotate the face away from the side being examined, based on the classification.

Patient #1:
Breadth measurement = 14 cm × 100 = 1400
Length measurement = 19 cm divided into 1400 = 73.6, which is equivalent to dolichocephalic, requiring that the face be rotated 50 degrees to the patient's left to correctly satisfy the above position.

Patient #2:
Breadth measurement = 16 cm × 100 = 1600
Length measurement = 18 cm divided into 1600 = 88.8, which is equivalent to brachycephalic, requiring that the face be rotated 36 degrees to the patient's left to correctly satisfy the above position.

To maximize positioning accuracy, it is absolutely essential to use an "angligner," "skull protractors," or other degree-calibrated accessories when positioning all skulls.

Because the majority of patients will be classified as mesocephalic, the routine positioning instructions in this book will be based on the average, adult-sized skull with the understanding that accurate measurements and skull classification must routinely be incorporated to achieve total success in craniographic positioning.

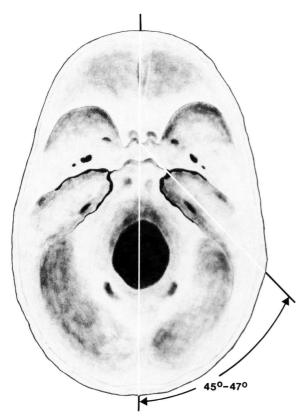

FIGURE 2-13. Cranial aspect, mesocephalic.

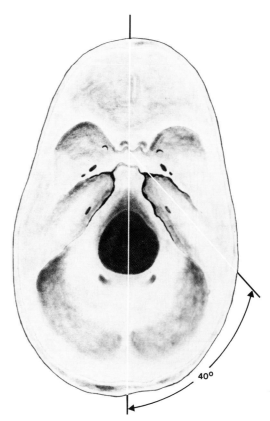

FIGURE 2-14. Cranial aspect, dolichocephalic.

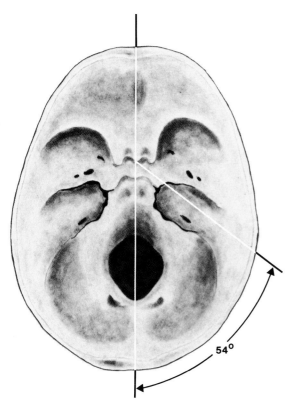

FIGURE 2-15. Cranial aspect, brachycephalic.

SKULL POSITIONING

3 UNIT

SKULL—ANTERIOR VIEW— ROUTINE
(Figs. 3-1 to 3-4)

PURPOSE. A posteroanterior projection to demonstrate the anterior cranial vault and the petrous regions projected into the orbital cavities.

POSITION. Place the patient in the prone or erect anterior position, with the midsagittal plane of the head perpendicular to and over the midline of the film holder. Place the patient's hands along the sides of the head for support. Rest the glabella and nose on the surface of the table or head unit, and flex the neck so that the canthomeatal line is perpendicular to the film surface.

PROJECTION. The central ray is projected perpendicularly, through the nasion, to the film surface.

TIMELY TIPS:
The orbital cavities can be demonstrated by using a true Caldwell's sinus view with a collimated projection centered at the nasion. (See page 101.)

Have cooperative patients assist in immobilization by holding radiolucent sponges against sides of the head.

A reverse of this projection will magnify the orbital cavities, thus revealing more of the central petrous portion.

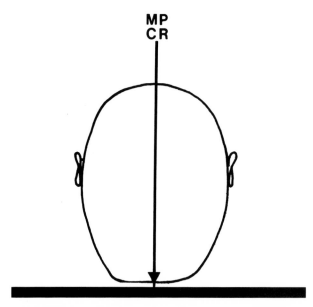

FIGURE 3-1. Skull, superior aspect, posteroanterior projection.

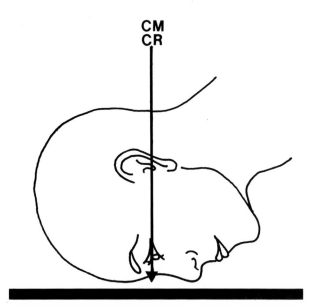

FIGURE 3-2. Skull, lateral aspect, posteroanterior projection.

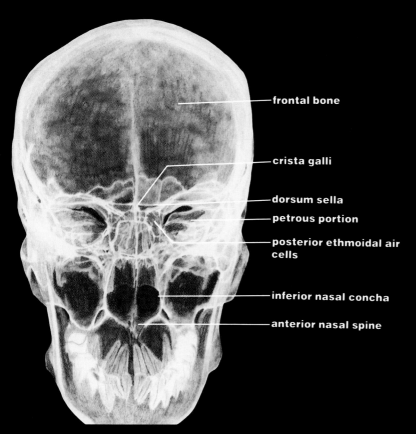

FIGURE 3-3. Skull, anterior view, routine.

VIEW: ANATOMIC DEMONSTRATION

- **Frontal bone, crista galli,** and **posterior ethmoidal air cells.**

- **Dorsum sellae, petrous portion** and **apices** filling orbital cavity, and medial portion of **carotid canal.**

- **Inferior nasal concha bones** and **anterior nasal spine.**

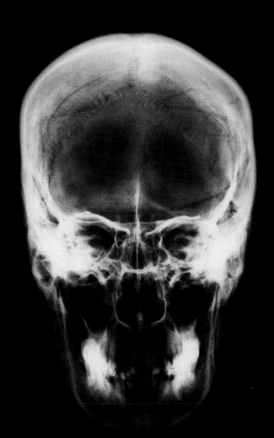

FIGURE 3-4. Skull, anterior view, routine.

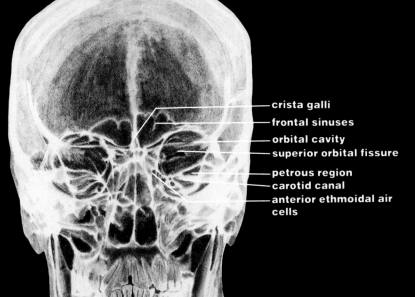

crista galli
frontal sinuses
orbital cavity
superior orbital fissure
petrous region
carotid canal
anterior ethmoidal air cells

FIGURE 3-5. Skull, anterior view, increased extension.

SKULL—ANTERIOR VIEW—COMPARISON STUDY SHOWING INCREASED EXTENSION
(Figs. 3-5 and 3-6)

- Increased extension of the neck or caudal projection will show the **petrous region** situated lower in the **orbital cavities,** with the **superior orbital fissures** well defined.

- The **frontal sinuses** and **crista galli** are also better defined.

- The **anterior ethmoidal air cells** begin to appear, whereas the posterior cells are obscured.

- **Petrous portion** is obscured.

CORRECTIVE ADJUSTMENT: Increase flexion at the neck **OR** decrease central ray projection approximately 10 degrees.

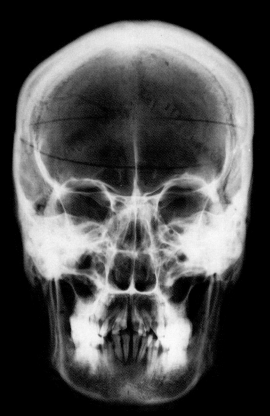

FIGURE 3-6. Skull, anterior view, increased extension.

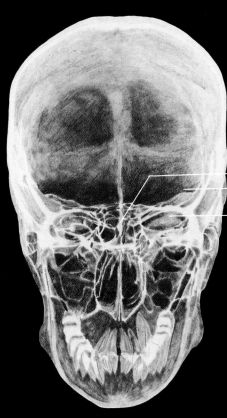

crista galli
arcuate eminence
petrous portion

FIGURE 3-7. Skull, anterior view, increased flexion.

SKULL—ANTERIOR VIEW—COMPARISON STUDY SHOWING INCREASED FLEXION
(Figs. 3-7 and 3-8)

- Increased flexion of the neck or increased cephalad projection will show the cranial vault elongated.

- **Arcuate eminences** will appear above the anterior floor of the cranial vault.

- **Frontal sinuses** and **crista galli** are obscured.

- Inferomedial aspect of **petrous portion** will appear in the orbital cavities.

CORRECTIVE ADJUSTMENT: Increase extension at the neck **OR** decrease central ray projection approximately 10 degrees.

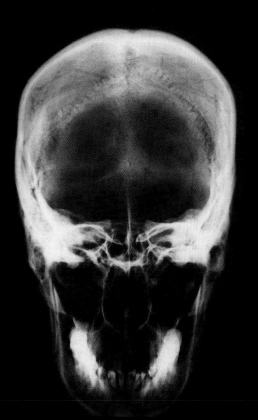

FIGURE 3-8. Skull, anterior view, increased flexion.

SKULL—LATERAL VIEW— ROUTINE
(Figs. 3-9 to 3-12)

PURPOSE. A lateral projection to demonstrate the walls of the cranial vault superimposed and a true profile of the sella turcica.

POSITION. From a prone or erect anterior position, turn the face away from the side being examined, resting the ear against the surface of the table or headboard. Rotate the body into an oblique position to ease the strain on the cervical spine. Manipulate the head, placing the midsagittal plane parallel, and the interpupillary line perpendicular, to the film surface. Flex the neck so that the canthomeatal line is perpendicular to the side of the table or headboard.

PROJECTION. The central ray is projected perpendicularly, through the sella turcica (average mesocephalic = ¾ in anterior and superior to the EAM on the canthomeatal line), to the film surface.

TIMELY TIPS:

Traumatic injuries to the head may necessitate bilateral views to demonstrate contrecoup fractures.

Translateral projections should be taken on supine, nonmanipulative, or unconscious patients, using parallel grid cassettes.

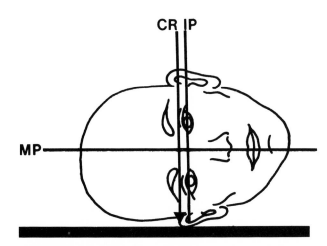

FIGURE 3-9. Skull, anterior aspect, lateral projection.

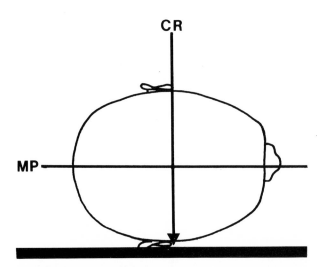

FIGURE 3-10. Skull, superior aspect, lateral projection.

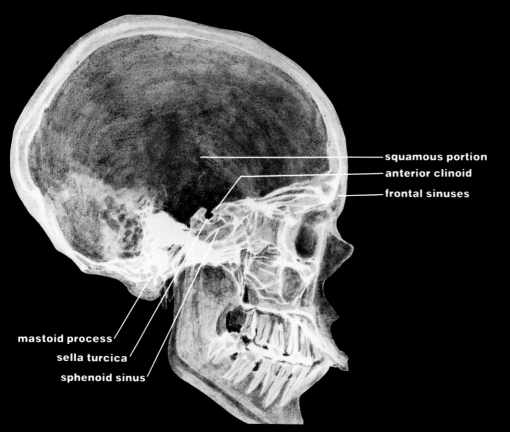

squamous portion
anterior clinoid
frontal sinuses

mastoid process
sella turcica
sphenoid sinus

FIGURE 3-11. Skull, lateral view, routine.

VIEW: ANATOMIC DEMONSTRATION

- Walls of the parietal bones, **squamous portion,** and **mastoid process** of temporal bones superimposed over counterparts.

- Lateral profile of the **sphenoid sinus** and **sella turcica.**

- **Anterior clinoid processes** should be superimposed.

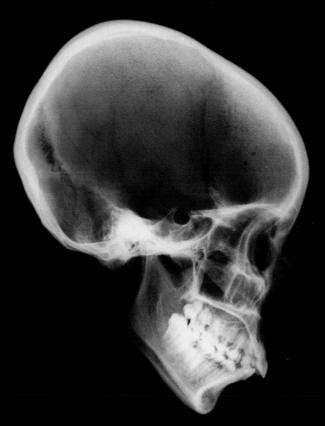

FIGURE 3-12. Skull, lateral view, routine.

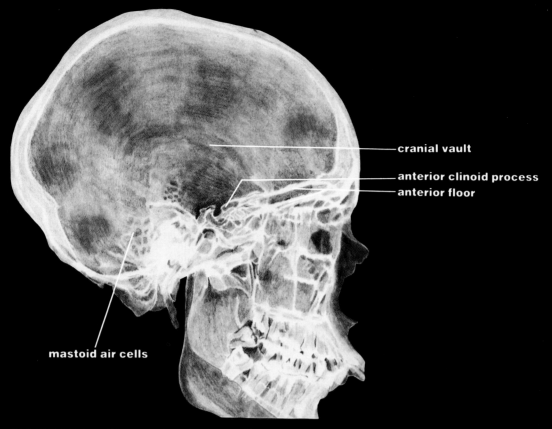

cranial vault

anterior clinoid process

anterior floor

mastoid air cells

FIGURE 3-13. Skull, lateral view, tilt.

SKULL—LATERAL VIEW— COMPARISON STUDY SHOWING INCREASED TILT (Figs. 3-13 and 3-14)

- Increased head tilt (sagging chin) or increased caudal projection will show an increased number of **superior mastoid air cells.**

- The upper, **anterior clinoid process** will be projected below the lower or opposite clinoid process.

- The two margins of the **anterior floor** of the **cranial vault** will be widely separated.

CORRECTIVE ADJUSTMENT: Support lateral mandible nearest film, aligning midsagittal plane parallel to film surface, **OR** decrease caudal central ray projection approximately 10 degrees.

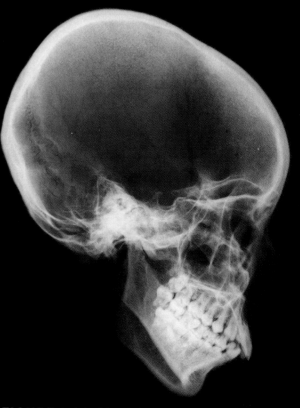

FIGURE 3-14. Skull, lateral view, tilt.

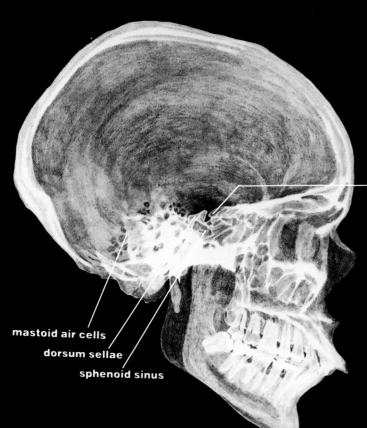

anterior clinoid process

mastoid air cells

dorsum sellae

sphenoid sinus

FIGURE 3-15. Skull, lateral view, rotation.

SKULL—LATERAL VIEW—
COMPARISON STUDY
SHOWING INCREASED
ROTATION
(Figs. 3-15 and 3-16)

- Increased head rotation (face toward film surface) will show the upper **mastoid air cells** adjacent to **dorsum sellae.**

- The lateral silhouette of the **sphenoid sinus** is ill defined because of double margins.

- The upper, **anterior clinoid process** will be projected anterior to the lower or opposite clinoid process.

- The triangular shape of the **petrous portion** will be widened considerably.

CORRECTIVE ADJUSTMENT: Rotate face away from film surface approximately 10 degrees so that total midsagittal plane is parallel to film surface.

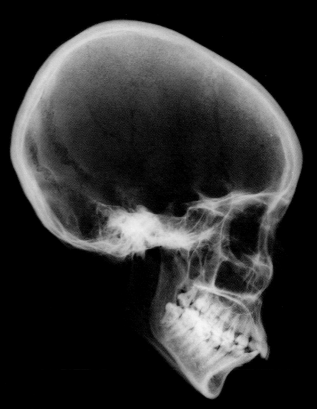

FIGURE 3-16. Skull, lateral view, rotation.

SKULL—OCCIPITAL VIEW (TOWNE)—ROUTINE (Figs. 3-17 to 3-20)

PURPOSE. An anteroposterior projection to demonstrate the occipital bone with the posterior clinoids and dorsum sellae within the foramen magnum.

POSITION. Place the patient in the supine or erect posterior position, with the midsagittal plane of the head perpendicular to and over the midline of the film holder. Flex the neck so that the canthomeatal line is perpendicular to the film surface.

PROJECTION. Locate the sella turcica on the side of the head. (Average mesocephalic = ¾ in anterior and superior to the EAM on canthomeatal line.) The central ray is projected 35 degrees caudad, through the sella turcica, to the film surface.

TIMELY TIPS:

For patients with limited flexion, rest the occiput on a grid cassette supported by a wedge sponge.

For patients in the prone or erect anterior position, rest the glabella on the table or headboard surface, with the canthomeatal line perpendicular to the film surface. The central ray is projected 35 degrees cephalad, through the sella turcica, to the film surface.

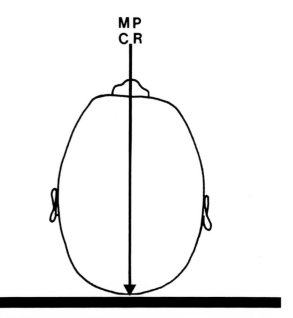

FIGURE 3-17. Skull, superior aspect, anteroposterior projection.

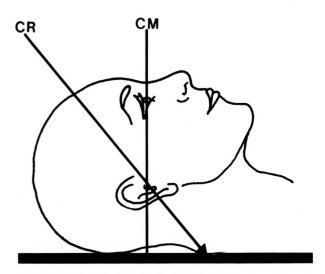

FIGURE 3-18. Skull, lateral aspect, anteroposterior projection.

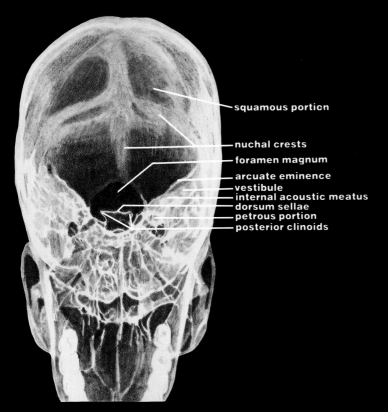

FIGURE 3-19. Skull, occipital (Towne) view, routine.

VIEW: ANATOMIC DEMONSTRATION

- **Squamous portion** with **nuchal crests** (slightly distorted).

- **Posterior clinoids** and **dorsum sellae** within the **foramen magnum.**

- **Petrous portions** with ridges, outline of **arcuate eminence,** and regions of the **vestibule** and **cochlea.**

- **Internal auditory canals** are visualized.

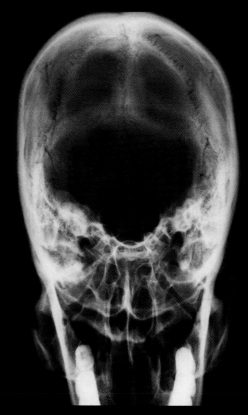

FIGURE 3-20. Skull, occipital (Towne) view, routine.

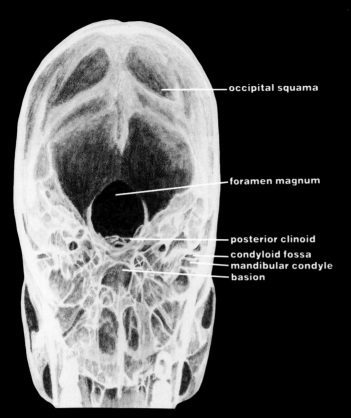

FIGURE 3-21. Skull, occipital view, increased caudal projection.

SKULL—OCCIPITAL VIEW— COMPARISON STUDY SHOWING INCREASED CAUDAL PROJECTION (Figs. 3-21 and 3-22)

- Increased flexion of the neck or caudal projection will show distortion of the **occipital squama** and enlargement of the **foramen magnum.**

- **Posterior clinoids** are nearly obscured in the region of the **basion.**

- This tangential view allows visualization of the **mandibular condyles** and the posterior walls of the **condyloid fossa.**

CORRECTIVE ADJUSTMENT: Increase extension at the neck **OR** decrease central ray projection approximately 10 degrees.

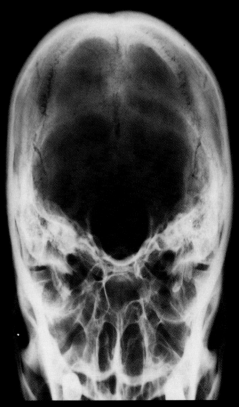

FIGURE 3-22. Skull, occipital view, increased caudal projection.

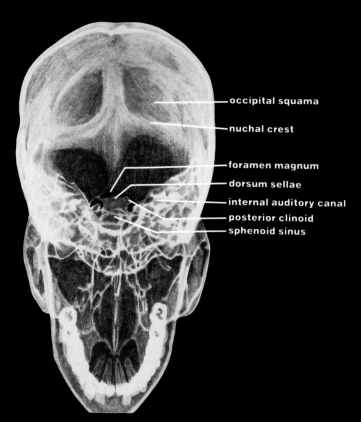

occipital squama

nuchal crest

foramen magnum

dorsum sellae

internal auditory canal

posterior clinoid

sphenoid sinus

FIGURE 3-23. Skull, occipital view, decreased caudal projection.

SKULL—OCCIPITAL VIEW— COMPARISON STUDY SHOWING DECREASED CAUDAL PROJECTION (Figs. 3-23 and 3-24)

- Increased extension of the neck or caudal projection will produce nondistorted view of the **occipital squama** and **nuchal crests.**

- **Posterior clinoids, dorsum sellae,** and a portion of the **sphenoid sinus** completely fill the posterior half of the **foramen magnum.**

- A view of the **foramen magnum** is limited to the posterior border.

- This view may be preferred over the routine view for better demonstration of the **internal auditory canals.**

CORRECTIVE ADJUSTMENT: Increase flexion at the neck **OR** increase central ray projection approximately 10 degrees.

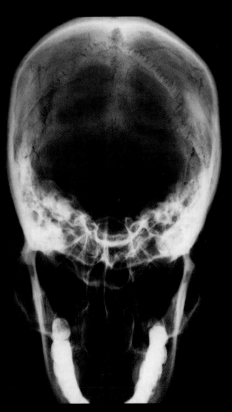

FIGURE 3-24. Skull, occipital view, decreased caudal projection.

SKULL—BASILAR VIEW—
ROUTINE
(Figs. 3-25 to 3-28)

PURPOSE. A submentovertical projection to demonstrate the floor of the cranial vault and its principal processes, foramina, and sinuses.

POSITION. Place the patient in the supine, elevated position (with 6-in cushion or positioning blocks) or erect posterior position, resting the vertex of the head against the table surface or head unit. If patient is supine, the knees should be flexed to reduce neck strain. Manipulate the head, placing the midsagittal plane perpendicular, and the infraorbital line parallel, to the film surface.

PROJECTION. The central ray is projected perpendicular to the infraorbital line, through a center point in line with the mandibular condyles, to the film surface.

TIMELY TIPS:

For patients with limited extension, rest the vertex of the head on a grid cassette supported by a wedge sponge. A strip of masking tape across the submental area connecting both sides of the cassette will help stabilize the patient.

This is an excellent view to demonstrate condylar fractures when the patient's mandible has been immobilized. For prone patients (verticosubmental projection), rest the extended chin on a grid cassette supported by a wedge sponge under the anterior chest. This view will produce good visualization of the basilar structures. However, it will provide more distortion, and the zygomatic arches will not be shown.

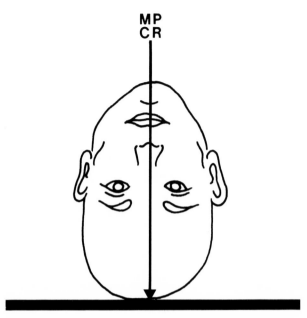

FIGURE 3-25. Skull, anterior aspect, sub-mentovertical projection.

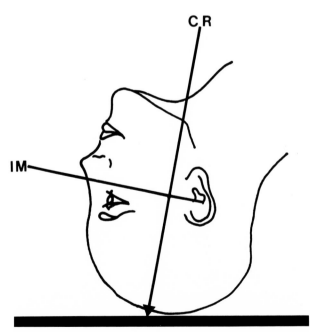

FIGURE 3-26. Skull, lateral aspect, sub-mentovertical projection.

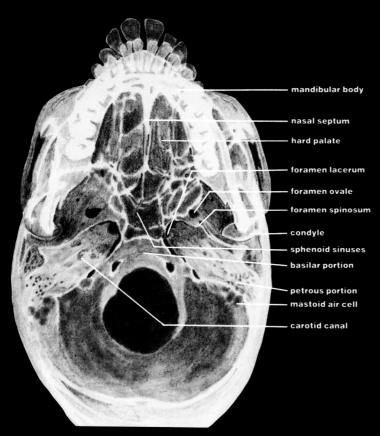

— mandibular body

— nasal septum

— hard palate

— foramen lacerum

— foramen ovale

— foramen spinosum

— condyle

— sphenoid sinuses

— basilar portion

— petrous portion

— mastoid air cell

— carotid canal

FIGURE 3-27. Skull, basilar view, routine.

VIEW: ANATOMIC DEMONSTRATION

- **Basilar portion** of occipital bone.

- **Petrous portion** of temporal bone, showing **carotid canal, foramen lacerum,** and **mastoid air cells.**

- Body of the sphenoid, showing the **sphenoid sinuses,** and the **foramen ovale** and **foramen spinosum** in the base of the greater wing.

- Region of the **posterior choanae, hard palate,** and **nasal septum.**

- Mandibular **body, neck,** and **condyles.**

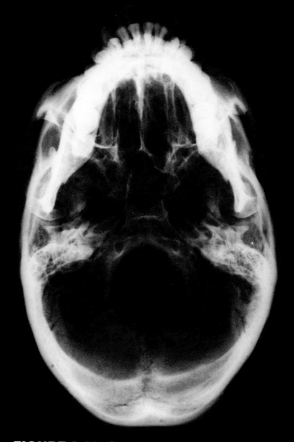

FIGURE 3-28. Skull, basilar view, routine.

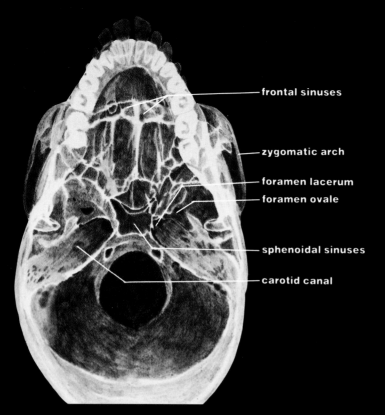

frontal sinuses

zygomatic arch

foramen lacerum

foramen ovale

sphenoidal sinuses

carotid canal

FIGURE 3-29. Skull, basilar view, increased extension.

SKULL—BASILAR VIEW— COMPARISON STUDY SHOWING INCREASED EXTENSION (Figs. 3-29 and 3-30)

- Increased extension of the neck or cephalad projection will distort the mandible beyond the frontal margin.

- The hard palate is partially obscured by the margins of the **frontal sinuses.**

- The **sphenoidal sinuses** remain well visualized, although the **foramen ovale** is reduced in size and the **foramen spinosum** is occluded.

- The **foramen lacerum** and the **carotid canal** are better visualized.

- Note that the **zygomatic arches** are emphasized.

CORRECTIVE ADJUSTMENT: Decrease extension at the neck **OR** decrease central ray projection approximately 10 degrees.

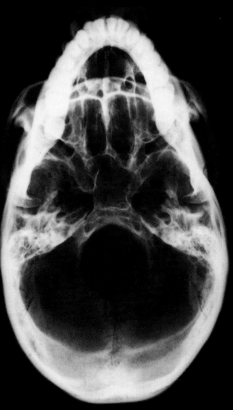

FIGURE 3-30. Skull, basilar view, increased extension.

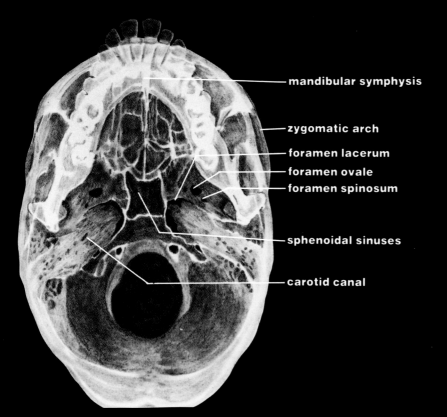

— mandibular symphysis

— zygomatic arch

— foramen lacerum
— foramen ovale
— foramen spinosum

— sphenoidal sinuses

— carotid canal

FIGURE 3-31. Skull, basilar view, increased flexion.

SKULL—BASILAR VIEW—COMPARISON STUDY SHOWING INCREASED FLEXION (Figs. 3-31 and 3-32)

- Increased flexion of the neck or decreased cephalad projection will show the **mandibular symphysis** superimposed over the frontal region and the anterior hard palate.

- The **sphenoidal sinuses, foramen ovale,** and **foramen spinosum** are well visualized.

- The **carotid opening** and **canal** become slightly occluded.

- The region of the **foramen lacerum** is slightly diminished.

- Note that the **zygomatic arches** are nearly obscured.

CORRECTIVE ADJUSTMENT: Increase extension at the neck **OR** increase cephalad central ray projection approximately 10 degrees.

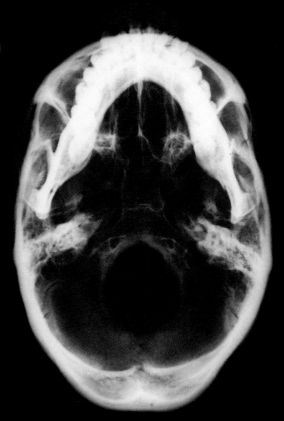

FIGURE 3-32. Skull, basilar view, increased flexion.

PETROUS POSITIONING

UNIT

PETROUS—POSTERIOR VIEW (ARCELIN)—ROUTINE
(Figs. 4-1 to 4-4)

PURPOSE. An anteroposterior projection to demonstrate the petrous portion of the temporal bone, with its long axis parallel to the film surface.

POSITION. Place the patient in a supine or erect posterior position, with the midsagittal plane of the head perpendicular to the film surface. For a mesocephalic skull, rotate the face 45 degrees away from the selected side. On the upper infraorbitomeatal line, center a point 1 in. anterior and superior to the EAM over the center of the film holder. Extend the chin slightly, aligning the infraorbitomeatal line perpendicular to the side of the film holder.

PROJECTION. The central ray is projected 15 degrees caudad, through the located upper point, to the center of the film holder.

TIMELY TIPS:

For a *brachycephalic* skull, rotate the face 36 degrees away from the selected side.

For a *dolichocephalic* skull, rotate the face 50 degrees away from the selected side.

Children may be immobilized with a strip of masking tape across the forehead, with each end adhered to the sides of the headboard or table.

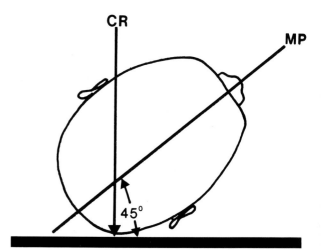

FIGURE 4-1. Petrous, cranial aspect, anteroposterior projection.

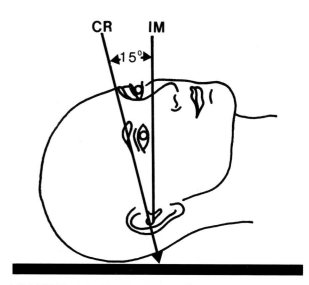

FIGURE 4-2. Petrous, oblique aspect, anteroposterior projection.

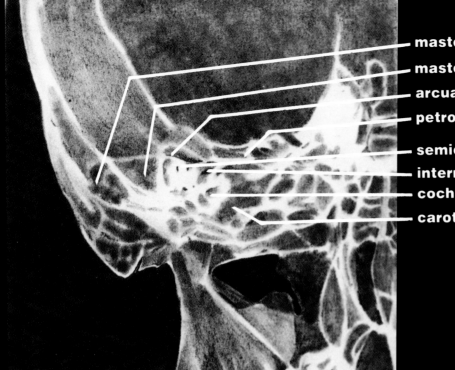

- mastoid air cell
- mastoid antrum
- arcuate eminence
- petrous ridge
- semicircular canal
- internal auditory canal
- cochlea
- carotid canal

FIGURE 4-3. Petrous, posterior (Arcelin) view, routine.

VIEW: ANATOMIC DEMONSTRATION

- **Mastoid air cells** and **mastoid antrum.**

- **Petrous ridge, arcuate eminence, semicircular canal, cochlea,** and **internal auditory canal.**

- **Petrous apex** and **carotid canal.**

- Note the clarity of the bony labyrinth area with a caudal projection of 10 to 15 degrees.

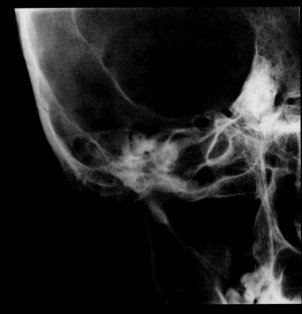

FIGURE 4-4. Petrous, posterior (Arcelin) view, routine.

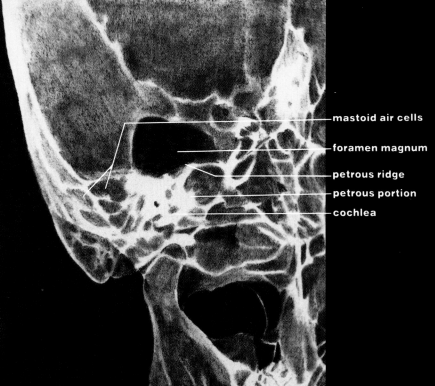

mastoid air cells

foramen magnum

petrous ridge

petrous portion

cochlea

FIGURE 4-5. Petrous, posterior view, increased caudal projection.

PETROUS—POSTERIOR VIEW—COMPARISON STUDY SHOWING INCREASED CAUDAL PROJECTION (Figs. 4-5 and 4-6)

- Increased central ray projection can be detected by the superimposition of the central petrous portion over the cervical vertebra and the projection of the **foramen magnum** superior to the **petrous ridge.**

- Therefore, the **vestibule, cochlea,** and **semicircular canals** are obscured.

- **Mastoid air cells** are visible but partially obstructed by the petrous base.

CORRECTIVE ADJUSTMENT: Decrease caudal projection 10 to 15 degrees.

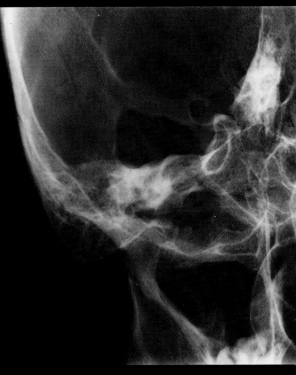

FIGURE 4-6. Petrous, posterior view, increased caudal projection.

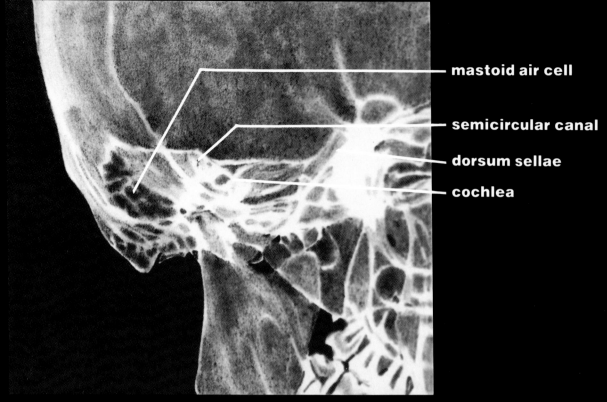

mastoid air cell

semicircular canal

dorsum sellae

cochlea

FIGURE 4-7. Petrous, posterior view, de-creased caudal projection.

PETROUS—POSTERIOR VIEW—COMPARISON STUDY SHOWING DECREASED CAUDAL PROJECTION (Figs. 4-7 and 4-8)

- Decreased central ray projection can be detected by the first cervical vertebra located below the petrous base and by the diminished profile of the **dorsum sellae.**

- The **mastoid air cells** are highly visible.

- Components of the bony labyrinth, the **vestibule, cochlea,** and **semicircular canals** are not as demonstrable due to minimal projection.

CORRECTIVE ADJUSTMENT: Increase caudal projection approximately 10 degrees.

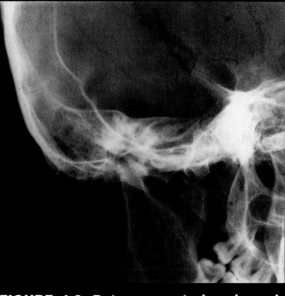

FIGURE 4-8. Petrous, posterior view, de-creased caudal projection.

PETROUS—ANTERIOR VIEW (STENVER)—ROUTINE
(Figs. 4-9 to 4-12)

PURPOSE. A posteroanterior projection to demonstrate the petrous portion of the temporal bone, with its long axis parallel to the film surface.

POSITION. Place the patient in a prone or erect anterior position, with the midsagittal plane of the head perpendicular to the film surface. For a *mesocephalic* skull, rotate the face 45 degrees away from the selected side. On the lower infraorbitomeatal line, center a point 1 in. anterior to the EAM over the center of the film holder. Extend the neck slightly, aligning the infraorbitomeatal line perpendicular to the side of the film holder.

PROJECTION. The central ray is projected 12 degrees cephalad, through the located lower point, to the center of the film holder.

TIMELY TIPS:

For a *brachycephalic* skull, rotate the face 36 degrees away from the selected side.

For a *dolichocephalic* skull, rotate the face 50 degrees away from the selected side.

Be very critical of head tilt when rotating the skull.

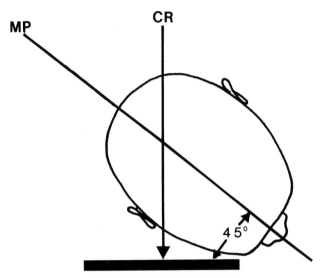

FIGURE 4-9. Petrous, cranial aspect, posteroanterior projection.

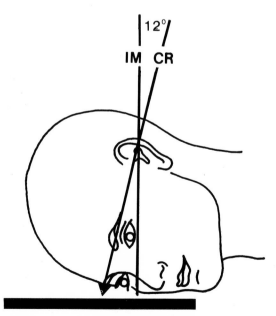

FIGURE 4-10. Petrous, oblique aspect, posteroanterior projection.

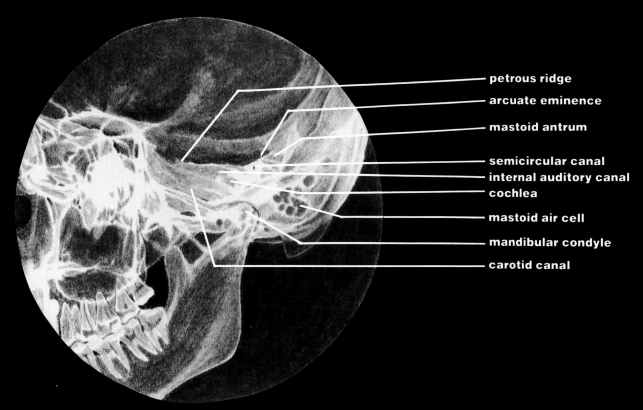

- petrous ridge
- arcuate eminence
- mastoid antrum
- semicircular canal
- internal auditory canal
- cochlea
- mastoid air cell
- mandibular condyle
- carotid canal

FIGURE 4-11. Petrous, anterior (Stenver) view, routine.

VIEW: ANATOMIC DEMONSTRATION

- **Mastoid air cells** and **mastoid antrum.**

- **Petrous ridge, arcuate eminence, semicircular canal, cochlea,** and **internal auditory canal.**

- **Petrous apex** and the **carotid canal.**

- Note the **mandibular condyle** centered below the **cochlea** and **superior semicircular canal.**

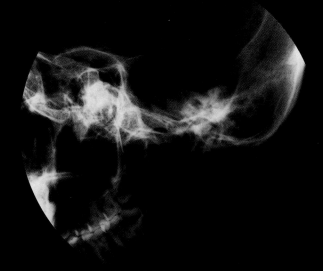

FIGURE 4-12. Petrous, anterior (Stenver) view, routine.

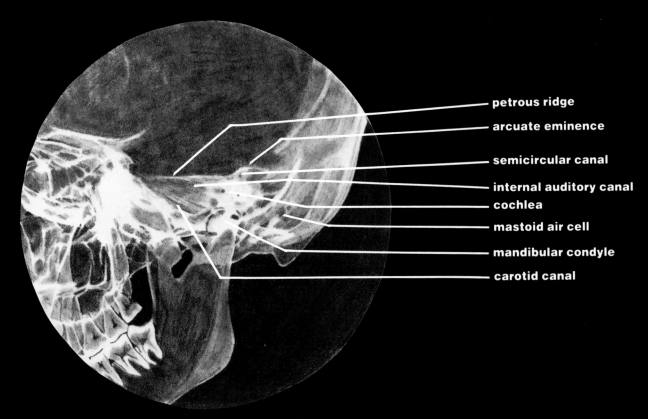

- petrous ridge
- arcuate eminence
- semicircular canal
- internal auditory canal
- cochlea
- mastoid air cell
- mandibular condyle
- carotid canal

FIGURE 4-13. Petrous, anterior view, increased rotation.

PETROUS—ANTERIOR VIEW— COMPARISON STUDY SHOWING INCREASED ROTATION (Figs. 4-13 and 4-14)

- Increased head rotation can be detected by the location of the lower **mandibular condyle** under and in line with the **cochlea.**

- Visibility of the **mastoid air cells** is narrowed slightly.

- The **petrous ridge, arcuate eminence,** and **semicircular canals** remain well visualized.

- The **cochlea** is slightly occluded, but the **internal auditory canal** remains well visualized.

- The **petrous apex** and **carotid canal** are relatively unchanged.

CORRECTIVE ADJUSTMENT: Decrease rotation of the face approximately 10 degrees.

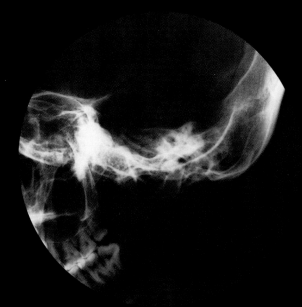

FIGURE 4-14. Petrous, anterior view, increased rotation.

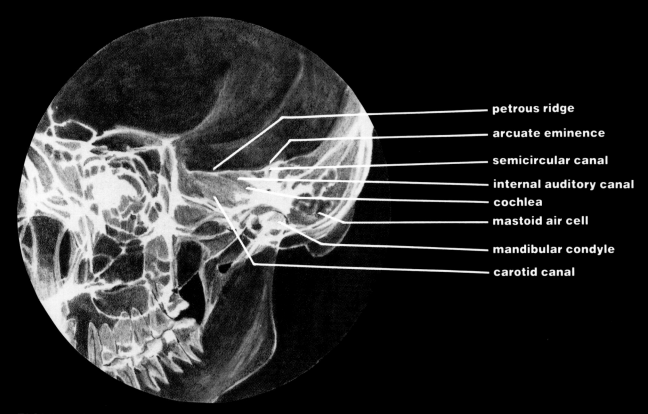

petrous ridge
arcuate eminence
semicircular canal
internal auditory canal
cochlea
mastoid air cell
mandibular condyle
carotid canal

FIGURE 4-15. Petrous, anterior view, decreased rotation.

PETROUS—ANTERIOR VIEW— COMPARISON STUDY SHOWING DECREASED ROTATION (Figs. 4-15 and 4-16)

- Decreased head rotation can be detected by the location of the lower **mandibular condyle** under and in line with the **arcuate eminence.**

- Region of the **mastoid air cells** is well visualized.

- The medial **petrous ridge** is foreshortened, although the **arcuate eminence** is lengthened.

- The superior **semicircular canal** becomes slightly occluded, and the internal definition of the **cochlea** is obscured.

- The **internal auditory canal** and **carotid canal** are defined.

CORRECTIVE ADJUSTMENT: Increase rotation of the face approximately 10 degrees.

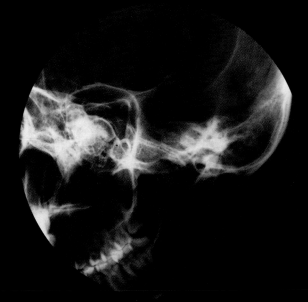

FIGURE 4-16. Petrous, anterior view, decreased rotation.

PETROUS—AXIAL VIEW (MAYER)—ROUTINE (Figs. 4-17 to 4-20)

PURPOSE. A semi-anteroposterior (axial) projection to demonstrate the petrous portion of the temporal bone, with its long axis perpendicular to the film surface.

POSITION. Prior to positioning, tape the auricle of each ear forward. Place the patient in a supine or erect posterior position, with the midsagittal plane of the head perpendicular to the film surface. For a *mesocephalic* skull, rotate the face 45 degrees toward the selected side. Center the adjacent EAM over the midline of the film holder; then flex the neck slightly, aligning the infraorbitomeatal line perpendicular to the side of the film holder.

PROJECTION. The central ray is projected 45 degrees caudad, through the lower EAM, to the film holder.

TIMELY TIPS:

For a *brachycephalic* skull, rotate the face 54 degrees toward the selected side.

For a *dolichocephalic* skull, rotate the face 40 degrees toward the selected side.

When using a floating table top, positioning accuracy may be enhanced by pre-aligning the angled central ray to the center of the film holder. Then, position the patient with positioning angligners, and move them into the central ray lineup.

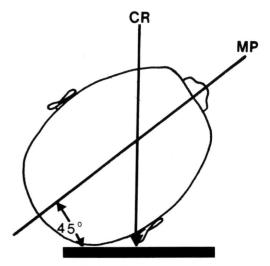

FIGURE 4-17. Petrous, cranial aspect, axial projection.

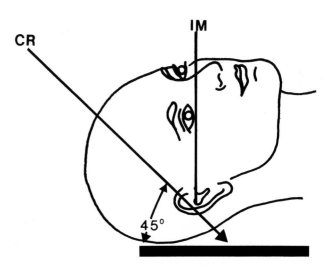

FIGURE 4-18. Petrous, oblique aspect, axial projection.

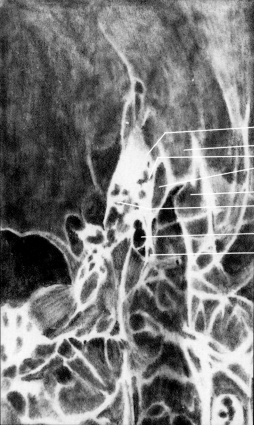

mastoid antrum
zygomatic air cell
tympanic cavity
external auditory canal
mandibular condyle
internal auditory foramen
carotid canal
foramen lacerum

FIGURE 4-19. Petrous, axial (Mayer) view, routine.

VIEW: ANATOMIC DEMONSTATION

- **Zygomatic air cells** and **mastoid antrum.**

- **External auditory canal, tympanic cavity,** and region of the **internal auditory foramen** and canal.

- **Carotid canal** and region of the **foramen lacerum.**

- **Mandibular condyle.**

FIGURE 4-20. Petrous, axial (Mayer) view, routine.

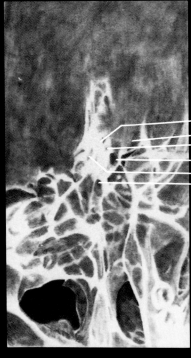

mastoid antrum
zygomatic air cell
tympanic cavity
external auditory canal
internal auditory foramen
carotid canal

FIGURE 4-21. Petrous, axial (Owen) view, decreased projection and increased rotation.

PETROUS—AXIAL VIEW (OWEN)—COMPARISON STUDY SHOWING DECREASED PROJECTION AND INCREASED ROTATION (Figs. 4-21 and 4-22)

- Decreased central ray angulation and slight increase in head rotation will show foreshortening of the long axis of the **petrous pillar.**

- **Zygomatic air cells** and **mastoid antrum** are visualized.

- **External auditory canal, tympanic cavity,** and region of the **internal auditory foramen** and canal are seen but very slightly modified.

- **Carotid canal** is visualized but slightly foreshortened.

- The region of the foramen lacerum is obscured by the lateral sella turcica.

CORRECTIVE ADJUSTMENT: To reposition for a routine *Mayer's* view, decrease head rotation 5 degrees and increase central ray angulation 10 degrees.

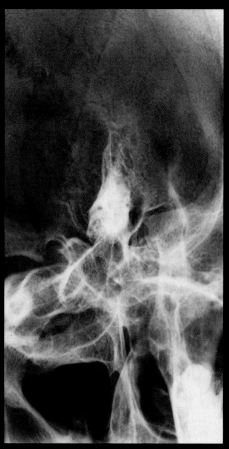

FIGURE 4-22. Petrous, axial (Owen) view, decreased projection and increased rotation.

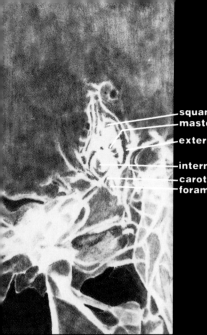

squamous air cell
mastoid antrum
external auditory canal
internal auditory foramen
carotid canal
foramen lacerum

FIGURE 4-23. Petrous, axial (Compere) view, decreased projection and increased rotation.

PETROUS—AXIAL VIEW (COMPERE)—COMPARISON STUDY SHOWING DECREASED PROJECTION AND INCREASED ROTATION (Figs. 4-23 and 4-24)

- Decreased central ray angulation and increased head rotation will show foreshortening of the long axis of the petrous pillar.

- **Squamous air cells** and **mastoid antrum** are diminished; however, they are visualized in truer design.

- **External auditory canal** is diminished, but the **internal auditory foramen** is better defined.

- **Carotid canal** is visualized but foreshortened.

- The region of the **foramen lacerum** is obscured by the posterior sphenoid body.

CORRECTIVE ADJUSTMENT: To reposition for a routine *Mayer's* view, decrease head rotation 15 degrees and increase central ray angulation 15 degrees.

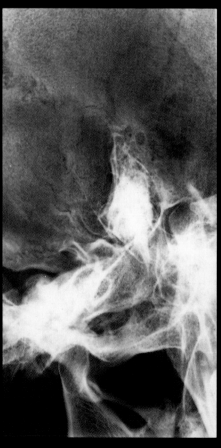

FIGURE 4-24. Petrous, axial (Compere) view, decreased projection and increased rotation.

PETROUS—LATERAL VIEW (LAW)—ROUTINE (Figs. 4-25 to 4-28)

PURPOSE. A lateral projection to demonstrate the mastoid regions and the internal and external auditory canals superimposed.

POSITION. Prior to positioning, tape the auricle of each ear forward. Place the patient in a prone or erect anterior position, with the midsagittal plane of the head parallel to the film surface. For a *mesocephalic* skull, rotate the face 15 degrees toward the selected side. Center a point 1 in. posterior to the adjacent EAM over the midline of the film holder; then adjust the head slightly, aligning the infraorbitomeatal line perpendicular to the side of the film holder.

PROJECTION. The central ray is projected 15 degrees caudad, through the lower point, to the film holder.

TIMELY TIPS:
For a *brachycephalic* skull, rotate the face 24 degrees toward the selected side. Central ray remains 15 degrees caudad.

For a *dolichocephalic* skull, rotate the face 10 degrees toward the selected side. Central ray remains 15 degrees caudad.

A comparable nongrid view may be obtained by placing the head in a true lateral position; then angle the tube 15 degrees caudad and 15 degrees anteriorly, through the lower point, to the film holder.

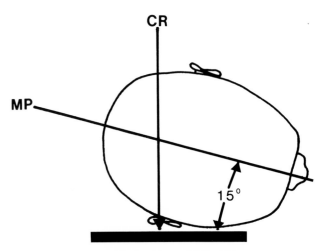

FIGURE 4-25. Petrous, cranial aspect, lateral projection.

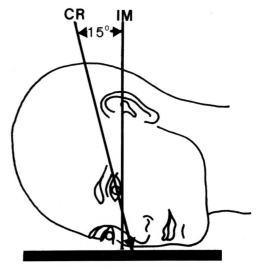

FIGURE 4-26. Petrous, oblique aspect, lateral projection.

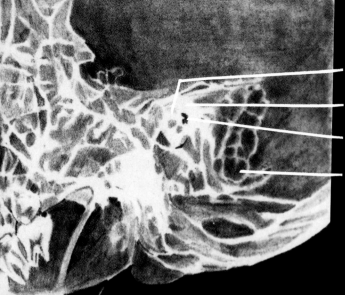

- epitympanic recess
- mastoid antrum
- external auditory canal
- mastoid air cell

FIGURE 4-27. Petrous, lateral (Law's) view, routine.

VIEW: ANATOMIC DEMONSTRATION

Mastoid antrum and **air cells.**

Superimposed **internal** and **external auditory canals.**

Region of the middle ear and the **epitympanic recess.**

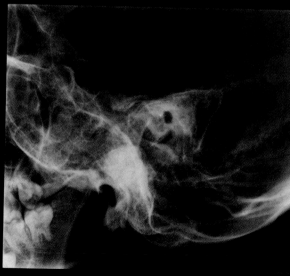

FIGURE 4-28. Petrous, lateral (Law's) view, routine.

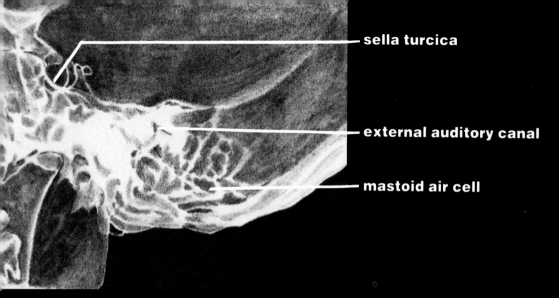

— sella turcica

— external auditory canal

— mastoid air cell

**FIGURE 4-29. Petrous, lateral view, de-
creased projection.**

PETROUS—LATERAL VIEW—
COMPARISON STUDY
SHOWING DECREASED
PROJECTION
(Figs. 4-29 and 4-30)

- Decreased central ray angulation will show the mastoid antrum obscured by superimposed air cells of the opposite side.

- **Mastoid air cells** are visible, with superior and inferior cells slightly obscured.

- **Internal** and **external auditory canal** superimposition is not visible.

- Regions of the middle ear and the epitympanic recess are not defined.

CORRECTIVE ADJUSTMENT: Increase central ray angulation 10 degrees.

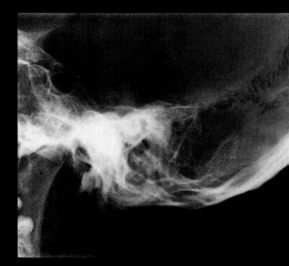

FIGURE 4-30. Petrous, lateral view, decreased projection.

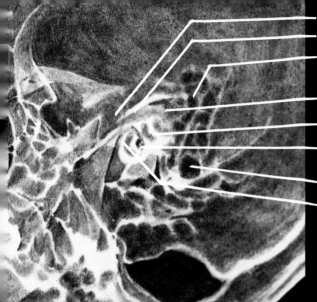

mandibular condyle
external auditory meatus
mastoid antrum

epitympanic recess
semicircular canals
internal auditory meatus

mastoid air cell
cochlea

FIGURE 4-31. Petrous, lateral (Schüller's) view, increased projection and decreased rotation.

PETROUS—LATERAL VIEW (SCHÜLLER)—COMPARISON STUDY SHOWING INCREASED PROJECTION AND NO ROTATION
(Figs. 4-31 and 4-32)

- A caudal central ray angulation of 25 degrees with a true lateral skull position will show the **mastoid antrum** well.

- **Mastoid air cells** are demonstrated in a slightly elongated pattern.

- Regions of the **internal** and **external auditory meatuses** are visualized separately.

- Regions of the **middle ear** and the **epitympanic recess** are visible.

CORRECTIVE ADJUSTMENT: To reposition for a routine *Law's* view, increase head rotation 15 degrees and decrease tube angulation 10 degrees.

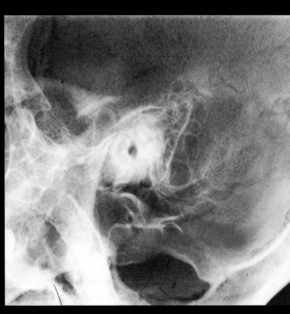

FIGURE 4-32. Petrous, lateral (Schüller's view, increased projection.

SINUS POSITIONING

UNIT 5

SINUSES—ANTERIOR VIEW OF MAXILLARY (WATER'S)— ROUTINE
(Figs. 5-1 to 5-4)

PURPOSE. An erect posteroanterior projection to demonstrate the maxillary sinuses above the petrous ridges and to demonstrate fluid level in the antra.

POSITION. Place the patient in an erect anterior position, with the midsagittal plane of the head perpendicular to the film surface. Extend the neck, resting on the chin, so that the canthomeatal line forms a 37-degree angle with the film surface.

PROJECTION. The central ray is projected horizontally and perpendicularly, through the anterior nasal spine, to the film surface.

TIMELY TIPS:
It is helpful to allow the patient to relax the neck after establishing your positioning lineup in order to reduce strain and subsequent motion. Then reposition immediately before making exposure.

Placing an extension cone or cylinder against the posterior skull will also help stabilize the patient and improve definition.

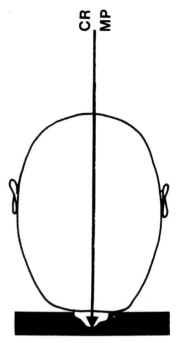

FIGURE 5-1. Sinuses, cranial aspect, posteroanterior projection.

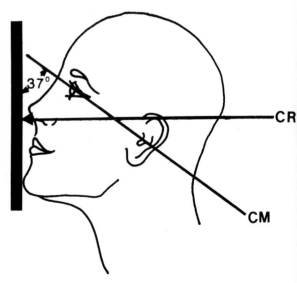

FIGURE 5-2. Sinuses, lateral aspect, posteroanterior projection.

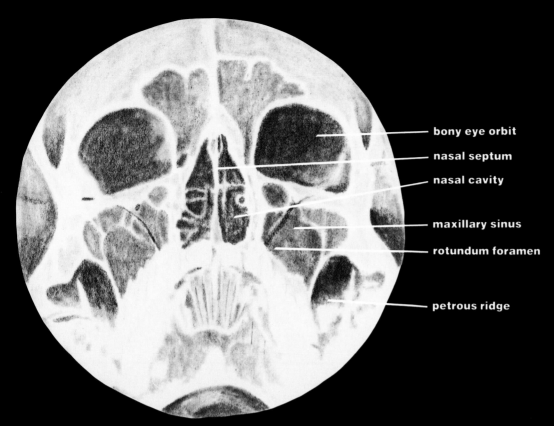

- bony eye orbit
- nasal septum
- nasal cavity
- maxillary sinus
- rotundum foramen
- petrous ridge

FIGURE 5-3. Sinuses, anterior (Water's) view, routine.

VIEW: ANATOMIC DEMONSTRATION

- **Maxillary sinuses** situated just superior to the **petrous ridge.**

- A distinct fluid line will appear when fluid is present.

- Nasal bones, **nasal septum,** and **nasal cavity.**

- Roof of the **bony eye orbits.**

- **Rotundum foramina** are slightly visible along the mid-medial walls of the **maxillary antra.**

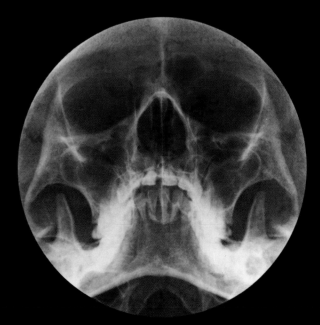

FIGURE 5-4. Sinuses, anterior (Water's) view, routine.

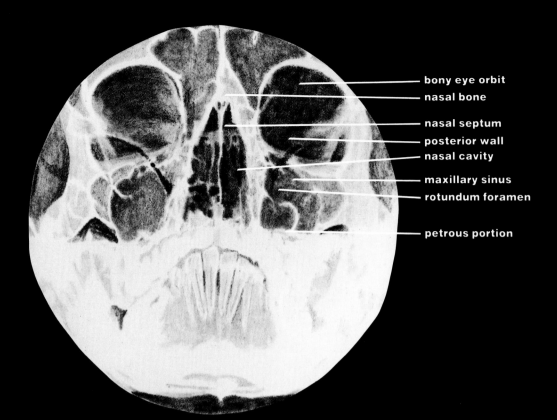

bony eye orbit
nasal bone

nasal septum
posterior wall
nasal cavity

maxillary sinus
rotundum foramen

petrous portion

FIGURE 5-5. Sinuses, anterior view, decreased extension.

SINUSES—ANTERIOR VIEW OF MAXILLARY— COMPARISON STUDY SHOWING DECREASED EXTENSION (Figs. 5-5 and 5-6)

- Decreased extension of the neck will show the **petrous portion** superimposed over the lower **maxillary sinuses.**

- Fluid lines may be obscured by the **petrous portion.**

- **Nasal bones, nasal septum,** and **nasal cavity** remain well visualized.

- Roof and posterior walls of the **bony eye orbits** are visualized.

- **Rotundum foramina** are better visualized in this view.

CORRECTIVE ADJUSTMENT: Increase extension of the neck 10 degrees.

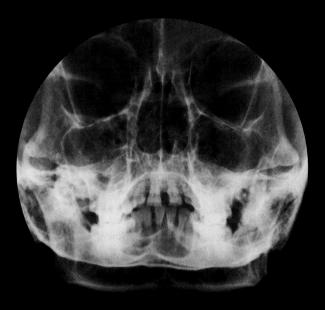

FIGURE 5-6. Sinuses, anterior view, decreased extension.

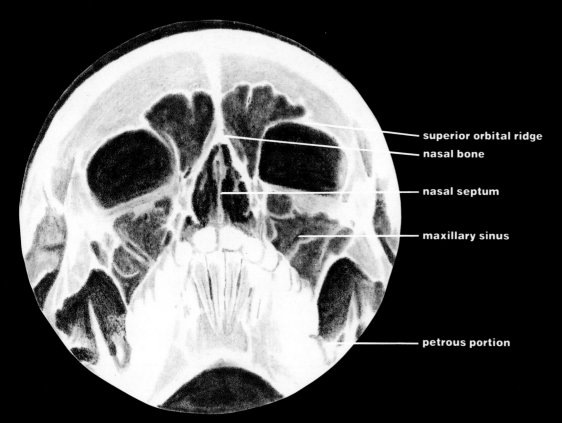

superior orbital ridge
nasal bone

nasal septum

maxillary sinus

petrous portion

FIGURE 5-7. Sinuses, anterior view, increased extension.

SINUSES—ANTERIOR VIEW OF MAXILLARY— COMPARISON STUDY SHOWING INCREASED EXTENSION (Figs. 5-7 and 5-8)

- Increased extension of the neck will show the **petrous portion** considerably below the **maxillary sinuses.**

- Fluid lines could be seen if fluid were present; however, definition of the antra is diminished because of increased magnification.

- **Nasal bones** and upper **nasal septum** and nasal cavity are visualized.

- **Superior orbital ridges** and roof of orbital cavities are visualized.

- **Rotundum foramina** are obscured.

CORRECTIVE ADJUSTMENT: Decrease extension of the neck 10 degrees.

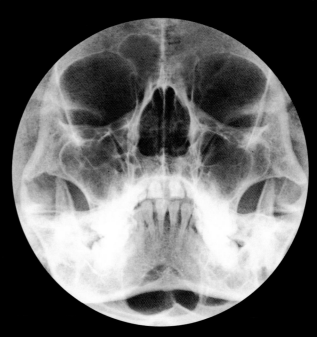

FIGURE 5-8. Sinuses, anterior view, increased extension.

SINUSES—ANTERIOR VIEW OF FRONTAL-ETHMOIDAL (CALDWELL)—ROUTINE (Figs. 5-9 to 5-12)

PURPOSE. A posteroanterior projection to demonstrate the frontal and anterior ethmoidal sinuses.

POSITION. Place the patient in a prone or erect anterior position, resting the forehead and nose on the table or headboard. The midsagittal plane and the canthomeatal line are perpendicular to the film surface.

PROJECTION. The central ray is projected 23 degrees caudad, through the nasion, to the film surface.

TIMELY TIPS:
For thin (hyposthenic) patients, support the anterior thorax with a pillow on positioning sponges.

For robust (hypersthenic) patients, complete suspended expiration will help reduce neck flexion to stabilize the position.

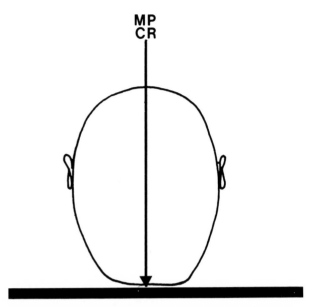

FIGURE 5-9. Sinuses, cranial aspect, posteroanterior projection.

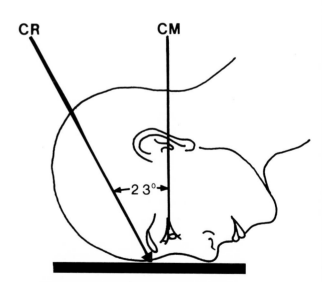

FIGURE 5-10. Sinuses, lateral aspect, posteroanterior projection.

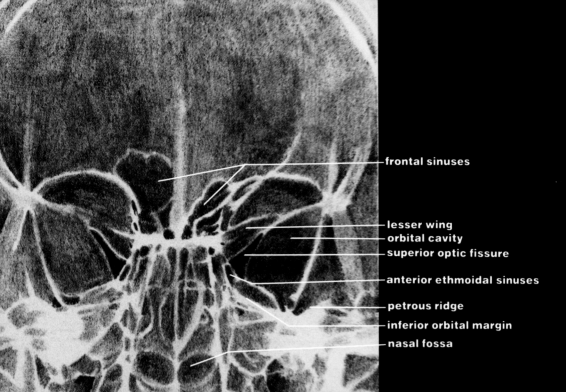

frontal sinuses

lesser wing
orbital cavity
superior optic fissure

anterior ethmoidal sinuses

petrous ridge
inferior orbital margin
nasal fossa

FIGURE 5-11. Sinuses, anterior (Cald-well's) view, routine.

VIEW: ANATOMIC DEMONSTRATION

- **Frontal sinuses** displayed in their entirety.

- **Anterior ethmoidal sinuses** on either side of the **nasal fossae.**

- **Lesser wings** of the sphenoid and **superior optic fissures.**

- **Posterior roof** and **wall** of the **orbital cavities.**

- **Petrous ridges** superimposed over the **inferior orbital margins.**

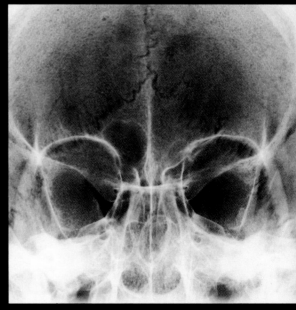

FIGURE 5-12. Sinuses, anterior (Cald-well's) view, routine.

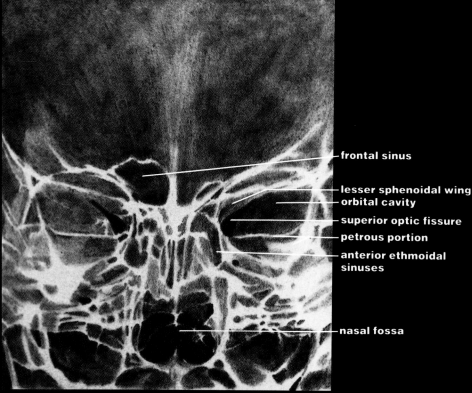

frontal sinus

lesser sphenoidal wing
orbital cavity

superior optic fissure

petrous portion

anterior ethmoidal
sinuses

nasal fossa

FIGURE 5-13. Sinuses, anterior view, decreased projection.

SINUSES—ANTERIOR VIEW OF FRONTAL-ETHMOIDAL— COMPARISON STUDY SHOWING DECREASED PROJECTION
(Figs. 5-13 and 5-14)

- Decreased central ray angulation will show the lower **frontal sinus** region obscured by the **lesser sphenoidal wings.**

- The **anterior ethmoidal sinuses** are better demonstrated on either side of the **nasal fossae.**

- The lesser wings of the sphenoid are narrowed; however, the **superior optic fissures** are fully demonstrated.

- The **petrous portions** will fill the lower half of the **orbital cavities.**

CORRECTIVE ADJUSTMENT. Increase caudal central ray angulation 10 degrees.

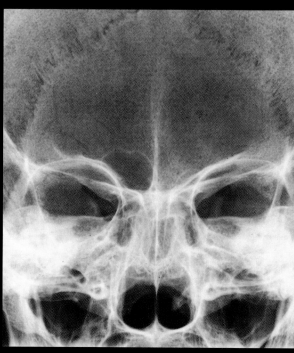

FIGURE 5-14. Sinuses, anterior view, decreased projection.

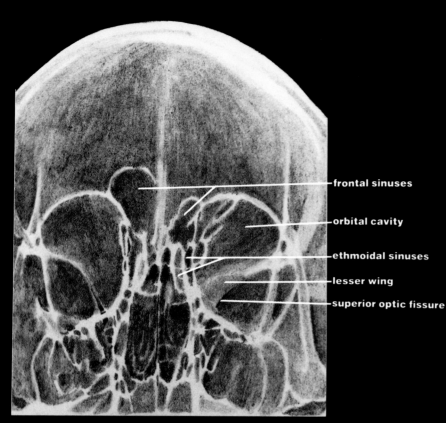

label column (right side of figure):
- frontal sinuses
- orbital cavity
- ethmoidal sinuses
- lesser wing
- superior optic fissure

FIGURE 5-15. Sinuses, anterior view, increased projection.

SINUSES—ANTERIOR VIEW OF FRONTAL-ETHMOIDAL— COMPARISON STUDY SHOWING INCREASED PROJECTION (Figs. 5-15 and 5-16)

- Increased central ray angulation will show the **frontal sinuses** distorted into an elongated design.

- The **ethmoidal sinuses** are mostly obscured.

- The **lesser wings** of the sphenoid and the **superior optic fissures** are distorted downward into the **orbital cavities.**

- The roofs of the **orbital cavities** are well visualized in this view.

- The petrous portions will be projected into the lower maxillary regions and not visualized.

CORRECTIVE ADJUSTMENT: Decrease caudal central ray angulation 10 degrees.

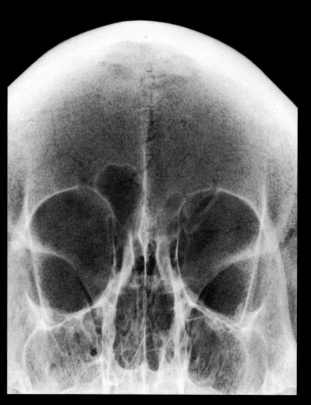

FIGURE 5-16. Sinuses, anterior view, increased projection.

SINUSES—OPEN-MOUTH VIEW OF SPHENOID (PIRIE)—ROUTINE
(Figs. 5-17 to 5-20)

PURPOSE. A posteroanterior projection to demonstrate the sphenoid sinus within the region of the open mouth.

POSITION. Place the patient in a prone or erect anterior position, with the midsagittal plane of the head perpendicular to and over the midline of the table. The patient must open the mouth as far as possible, resting the nose and chin over the center of the film holder.

PROJECTION. Locate the sella turcica on the side of the head. (Average mesocephalic = ¾ in anterior and superior to the EAM on the canthomeatal line.) Direct the central ray approximately 23 degrees caudad, through the sella turcica and the center of the open mouth, to the center of the film holder.

TIMELY TIPS:

The exact degree of central ray angulation will depend on the location of sella turcica in relation to the open mouth.

It is helpful to allow the patient to relax the mandible momentarily after establishing your positioning lineup in order to reduce strain and subsequent motion. Then reposition immediately before making exposure.

An alternate view of the sphenoid sinuses (verticosubmental—Schüller) may be taken with the patient's chin extended and resting on an elevated film holder.

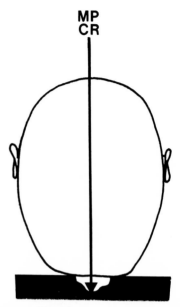

FIGURE 5-17. Sinuses, cranial aspect, posteroanterior projection.

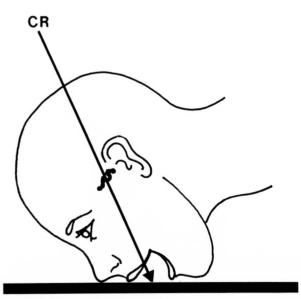

FIGURE 5-18. Sinuses, lateral aspect, posteroanterior projection.

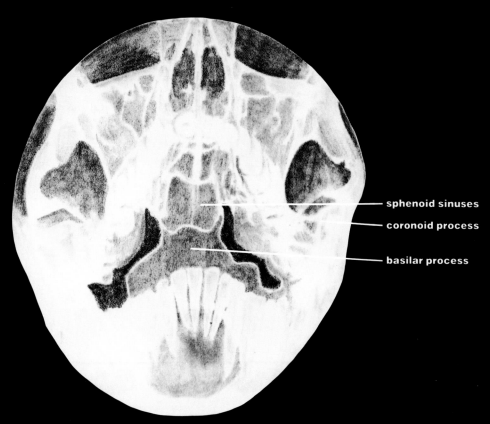

sphenoid sinuses

coronoid process

basilar process

FIGURE 5-19. Sinuses, open-mouth (Pirie) view, routine.

VIEW: ANATOMIC DEMONSTRATION

- **Sphenoid sinuses** within the region of the open mouth.

- **Basilar process** of occipital bone.

- Anterior view of the **coronoid processes** of the mandible.

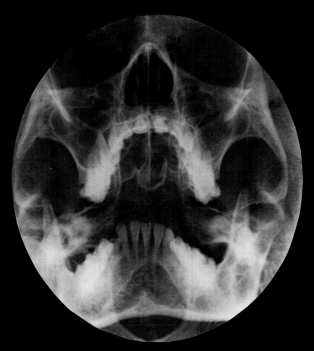

FIGURE 5-20. Sinuses, open-mouth (Pirie) view, routine.

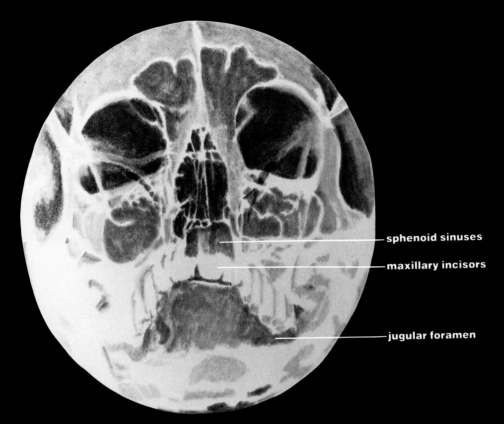

sphenoid sinuses

maxillary incisors

jugular foramen

FIGURE 5-21. Sinuses, open-mouth view, decreased projection.

SINUSES—OPEN-MOUTH VIEW OF SPHENOID— COMPARISON STUDY SHOWING DECREASED PROJECTION (Figs. 5-21 and 5-22)

- Decreased central ray angulation will show the **sphenoid sinuses** superimposed over the **maxillary incisors.**

- The **jugular foramina** are demonstrated in the space between the upper and lower molars.

- The coronoid processes of the mandible are obscured.

CORRECTIVE ADJUSTMENT: Increase central ray angulation 10 degrees.

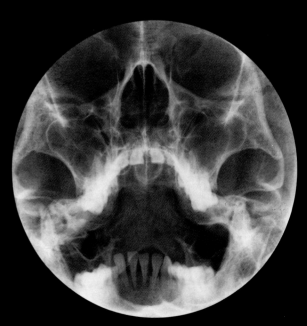

FIGURE 5-22. Sinuses, open-mouth view, decreased projection.

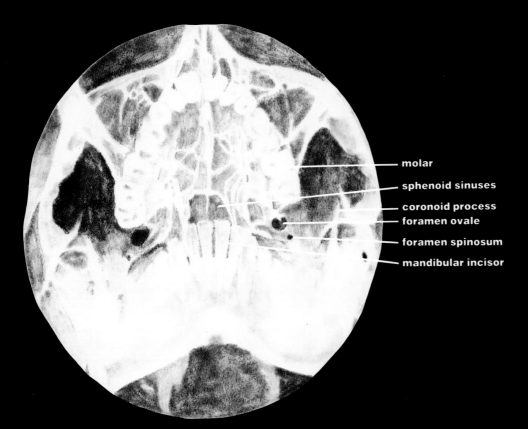

- molar
- sphenoid sinuses
- coronoid process
- foramen ovale
- foramen spinosum
- mandibular incisor

FIGURE 5-23. Sinuses, open-mouth view, increased projection.

SINUSES—OPEN-MOUTH VIEW OF SPHENOID— COMPARISON STUDY SHOWING INCREASED PROJECTION (Figs. 5-23 and 5-24)

- Increased central ray angulation will show the posterior **sphenoid sinuses** superimposed over the **mandibular incisors.**

- The basilar process of the occipital bone is obscured by the mandible.

- The **foramina ovale** and **spinosae** are well demonstrated in the space between the upper and lower **molars.**

- The **coronoid processes** of the mandible are well demonstrated.

CORRECTIVE ADJUSTMENT: Decrease central ray angulation 10 degrees.

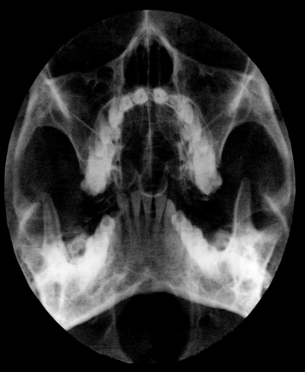

FIGURE 5-24. Sinuses, open-mouth view, increased projection.

SINUSES—LATERAL VIEW—ROUTINE
(Figs. 5-25 to 5-28)

PURPOSE. A lateral projection to demonstrate the four paranasal sinuses.

POSITION. Place the patient in a prone or erect right anterior oblique position, with the midsagittal plane of the head parallel to the film surface. Flex the neck to align the canthomeatal line perpendicular to side of the table or headboard. Support the side of chin with the patient's fist or positioning sponge.

PROJECTION. Direct the central ray perpendicularly, through a point ½ in posterior to the outer canthus of the eye, to the center of the film holder.

TIMELY TIPS:

Contrast in the sinus regions may be reduced by using nongrid techniques and accessories.

Care must be maintained to obtain true laterality for this particular view to eliminate superimposition of unwanted structures.

Use the vertical edge of a plastic right triangle to align perpendicularity of the interpupillary line in order to eliminate head tilt.

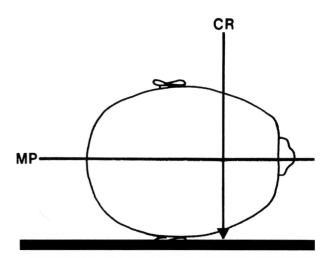

FIGURE 5-25. Sinuses, cranial aspect, lateral projection.

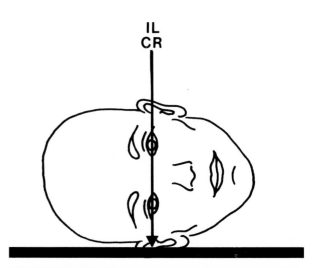

FIGURE 5-26. Sinuses, anterior aspect, lateral projection.

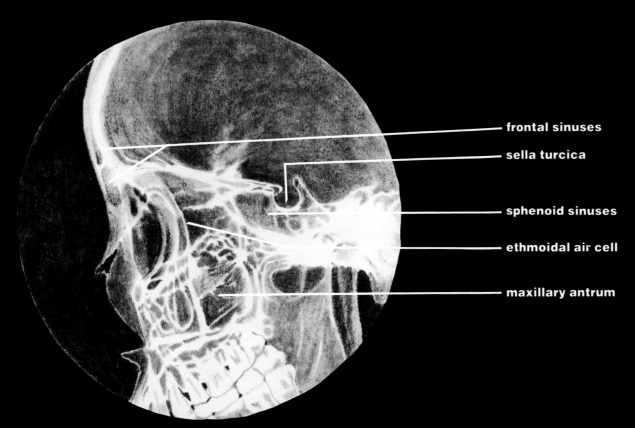

- frontal sinuses
- sella turcica
- sphenoid sinuses
- ethmoidal air cell
- maxillary antrum

FIGURE 5-27. Sinuses, lateral view, routine.

VIEW: ANATOMIC DEMONSTRATION

- **Sphenoid sinuses** within the body of sphenoid bone with a single-margin **sella turcica.**

- **Frontal sinuses** posterior to the glabella.

- **Ethmoidal air cells** directly superimposed on opposite air cells.

- **Maxillary antrum** directly superimposed on opposite antrum.

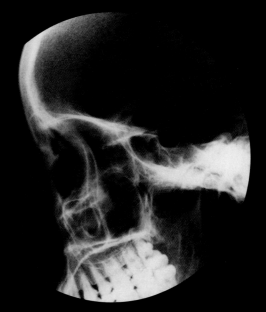

FIGURE 5-28. Sinuses, lateral view, routine.

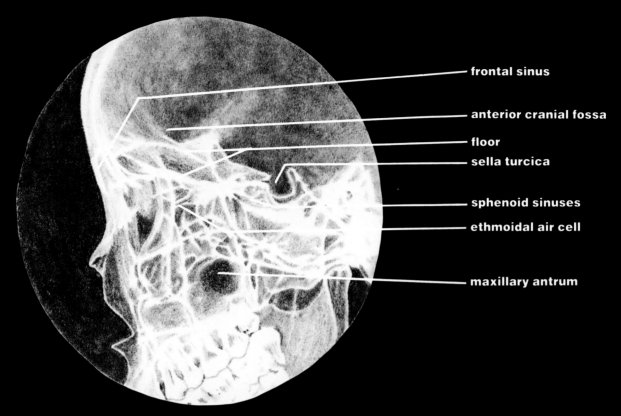

frontal sinus

anterior cranial fossa

floor

sella turcica

sphenoid sinuses

ethmoidal air cell

maxillary antrum

FIGURE 5-29. Sinuses, lateral view, increased tilt.

SINUSES—LATERAL VIEW—COMPARISON STUDY SHOWING TILT
(Figs. 5-29 and 5-30)

- Slight head tilt will show one lateral margin of the **sella turcica** below or above the opposite margin, which in turn will show occlusion of the **sphenoid sinuses.**

- A double line will appear in the floor of the **anterior cranial fossae.**

- The **frontal sinus** (anterior lobe) will lose marginal definition.

- **Ethmoidal air cells** will be partially occluded because of superimposition of facial structures.

- **Maxillary antra** will be partially occluded because of superimposition of facial structures.

CORRECTIVE ADJUSTMENT: Decrease head tilt 10 degrees by using right triangle or angligner in line with the interpupillary line.

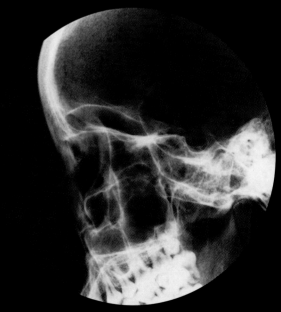

FIGURE 5-30. Sinuses, lateral view, increased tilt.

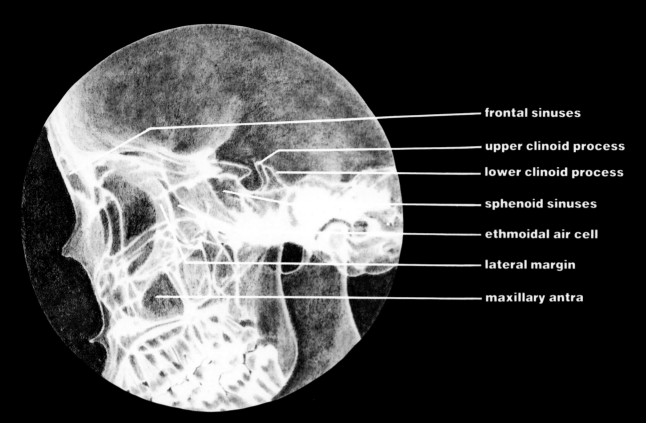

frontal sinuses

upper clinoid process

lower clinoid process

sphenoid sinuses

ethmoidal air cell

lateral margin

maxillary antra

FIGURE 5-31. Sinuses, lateral view, increased rotation.

SINUSES—LATERAL VIEW— COMPARISON STUDY SHOWING INCREASED ROTATION (Figs. 5-31 and 5-32)

- Slightly increased head rotation (face toward film surface) will show the **upper clinoid processes** projected anterior to the **lower clinoid processes.**

- The lateral silhouette of the **sphenoid sinuses** is ill defined due to double margins.

- The upper lateral lobe of the **frontal sinuses** will become more clearly defined.

- Some **ethmoidal air cells** will be visualized between the lateral margins of the bony eye orbits.

- The **maxillary antra** are partially occluded due to double margins.

CORRECTIVE ADJUSTMENT: Decrease head rotation 10 degrees.

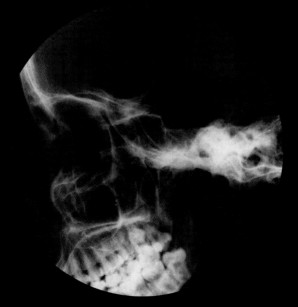

FIGURE 5-32. Sinuses, lateral view, increased rotation.

FACIAL BONE POSITIONING

UNIT 6

FACIAL BONES—ANTERIOR VIEW OF ORBITAL RIDGES (WATER'S)—ROUTINE (Figs. 6-1 to 6-4)

PURPOSE. A posteroanterior projection that will demonstrate the anterior facial bone structures.

POSITION. Place the patient in the prone or erect anterior position, with the midsagittal plane of the head perpendicular to and over the midline of the film holder. Place the patient's hands along the sides of the head for support. Adjust the head so that the canthomeatal line forms a 37-degree angle with the film surface.

PROJECTION. The central ray is projected perpendicularly, through the anterior nasal spine, to the film surface.

TIMELY TIPS:

For supine patients who cannot be moved, place a grid cassette beneath the occiput, and direct the central ray 40 degrees cephalad to the canthomeatal line, through the central incisors, to the film surface.

Trauma to the inferior orbital cavity or maxillary region may necessitate obtaining erect views for fluid level studies.

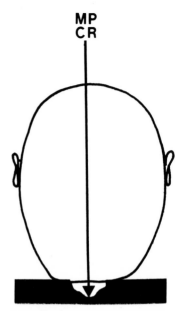

FIGURE 6-1. Facial bones, cranial aspect, posteroanterior projection.

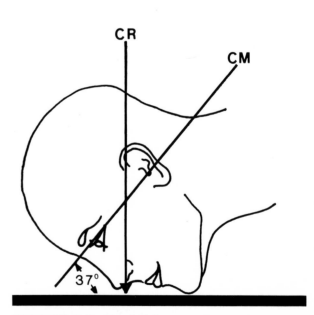

FIGURE 6-2. Facial bones, lateral aspect, posteroanterior projection.

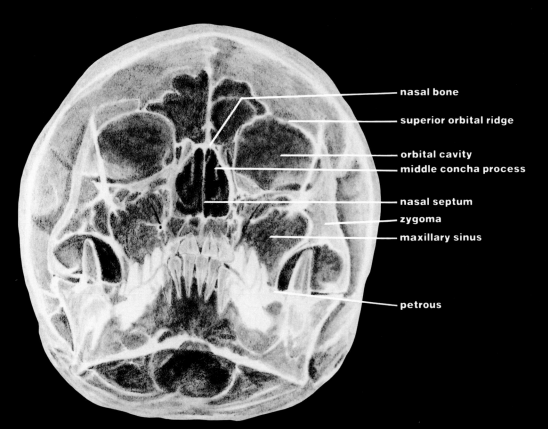

- nasal bone
- superior orbital ridge
- orbital cavity
- middle concha process
- nasal septum
- zygoma
- maxillary sinus
- petrous

FIGURE 6-3. Facial bones, anterior (Water's) view, routine.

VIEW: ANATOMIC DEMONSTRATION

- **Superior orbital ridges** and roofs of the **orbital cavities.**

- **Nasal bones, nasal septum,** and **middle concha processes.**

- **Maxillary bones** with **sinuses** and adjacent **zygomas.**

- Note that the **petrous ridges** are situated just below the **maxillary sinuses.**

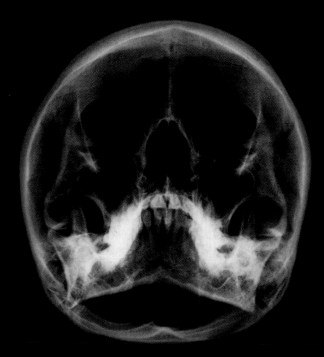

FIGURE 6-4. Facial bones, anterior (Water's) view, routine.

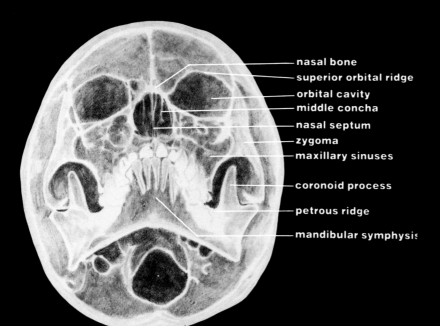

FIGURE 6-5. Facial bones, anterior view, increased extension.

FACIAL BONES—ANTERIOR VIEW OF ORBITAL RIDGES— COMPARISON STUDY SHOWING INCREASED EXTENSION (Figs. 6-5 and 6-6)

- Increased extension of the neck will show the **orbital cavities** reduced in size.

- The **superior orbital ridges** and roofs of the **orbital cavities** will still be seen, with slight lack of marginal sharpness because of increased object-film distance.

- **Nasal bones** and superior portion of **nasal septum** are visualized, but inferior portions of **middle concha** processes are obscured by the floor of the nasal cavity.

- **Maxillary bones, sinuses,** and adjacent **zygomas** will be seen with loss of detail.

- The **mandibular symphysis** and **coronoid processes** are demonstrated.

- Note that the **petrous ridges** are situated well below the **maxillary sinuses.**

CORRECTIVE ADJUSTMENT: Increase flexion at the neck 10 degrees.

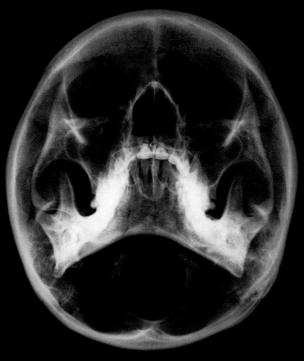

FIGURE 6-6. Facial bones, anterior view, increased extension.

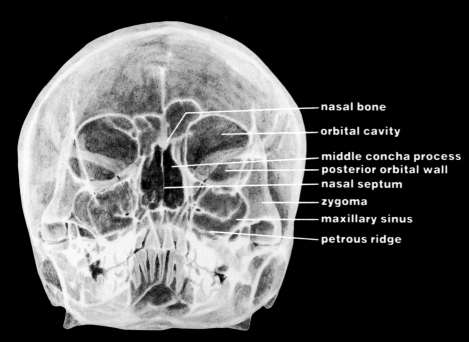

nasal bone
orbital cavity
middle concha process
posterior orbital wall
nasal septum
zygoma
maxillary sinus
petrous ridge

FIGURE 6-7. Facial bones, anterior view, increased flexion.

FACIAL BONES—ANTERIOR VIEW OF ORBITAL RIDGES— COMPARISON STUDY SHOWING INCREASED FLEXION
(Figs. 6-7 and 6-8)

- Increased flexion of the neck will show the **orbital cavities** enlarged to truer diameters.

- The orbital ridges and roofs of the **orbital cavities** will be demonstrated, and the lesser sphenoid wing and **posterior orbital walls** will appear.

- The **nasal bones, nasal septum,** and **middle concha processes** are demonstrated.

- The upper **maxillary bones** with **sinuses** and **zygomas** are demonstrated.

- Note that the **petrous ridges** are superimposed over the lower **maxillary antra.**

CORRECTIVE ADJUSTMENT: Increase extension at the neck 10 degrees.

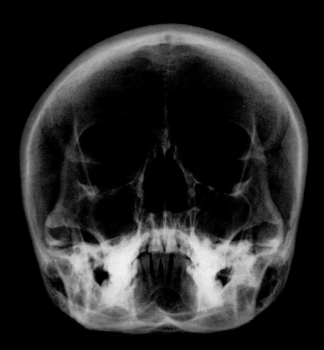

FIGURE 6-8. Facial bones, anterior view, increased flexion.

FACIAL BONES—LATERAL VIEW—ROUTINE
(Figs. 6-9 to 6-12)

PURPOSE. A lateral projection to demonstrate the facial bones superimposed in a true lateral profile.

POSITION. From a prone or erect anterior position, turn the face away from the side being examined, resting the ear against the table or headboard. Rotate the body into an oblique position to ease the strain on the cervical spine. Manipulate the head to place the midsagittal plane parallel, and the interpupillary line perpendicular, to the film surface. Flex the neck so that the canthomeatal line is perpendicular to the side of the table or headboard.

PROJECTION. The central ray is projected perpendicularly, through a point ½ in posterior to the outer canthus, to the center of the film surface.

TIMELY TIPS:

Better visualization of the superimposed facial bones may sometimes be obtained through stereo views incorporating a longitudinal tube shift.

Soft tissue structures can best be demonstrated with nongrid technique and an extension cone.

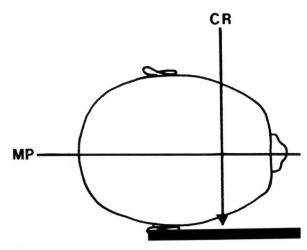

FIGURE 6-9. Facial bones, cranial aspect, lateral projection.

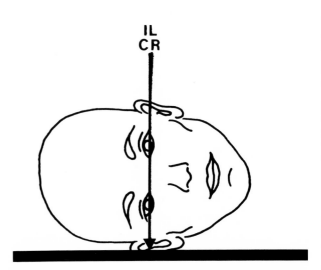

FIGURE 6-10. Facial bones, anterior aspect, lateral projection.

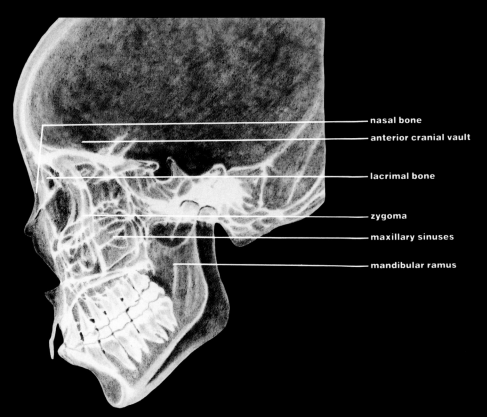

nasal bone

anterior cranial vault

lacrimal bone

zygoma

maxillary sinuses

mandibular ramus

FIGURE 6-11. Facial bones, lateral view, routine.

VIEW: ANATOMIC DEMONSTRATION

- **Nasal** and **lacrimal** bones will be superimposed over their counterparts.

- **Zygomatic bones** showing double silhouettes will be superimposed over **maxillary sinuses.**

- The floor of the **anterior cranial vault** will be demonstrated as a single silhouette.

- Note that the posterior margins and angles of the **mandibular rami** will not be superimposed because of projection by divergent rays.

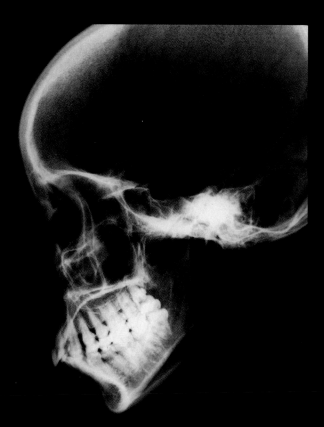

FIGURE 6-12. Facial bones, lateral view, routine.

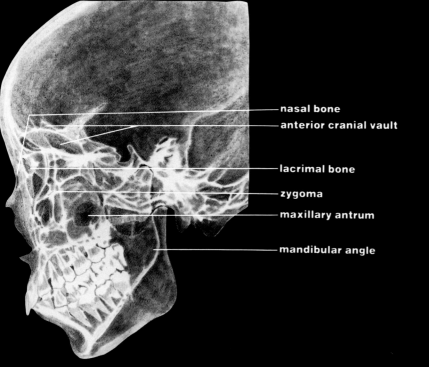

- nasal bone
- anterior cranial vault
- lacrimal bone
- zygoma
- maxillary antrum
- mandibular angle

FIGURE 6-13. Facial bones, lateral view, increased tilt.

FACIAL BONES—LATERAL VIEW—COMPARISON STUDY SHOWING INCREASED TILT (Figs. 6-13 and 6-14)

- Increased head tilt will allow the nasal and **lacrimal bones** to remain visualized with minimal distortion.

- The **zygomatic bones** will be nearly superimposed because of projection, thus revealing a portion of the **posterior maxillary antra.**

- The floor of the **anterior cranial vault** will demonstrate two margins.

- Note the increased distance between the **mandibular angles.**

CORRECTIVE ADJUSTMENT: Support lateral mandible nearest film, aligning midsagittal plane parallel to film surface, **OR** decrease caudal central ray projection approximately 10 degrees.

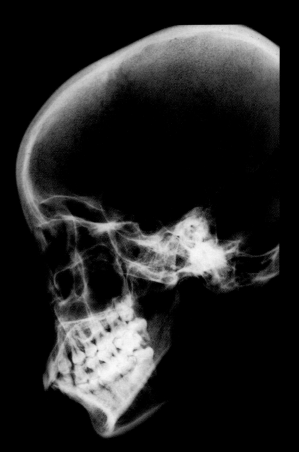

FIGURE 6-14. Facial bones, lateral view, increased tilt.

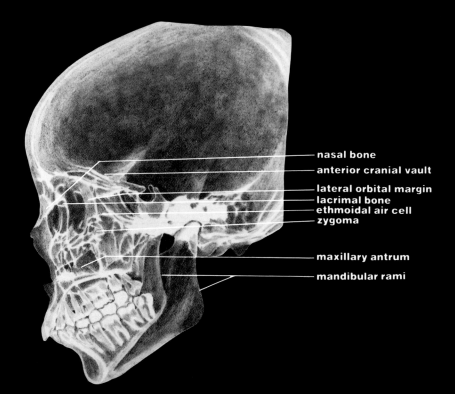

- nasal bone
- anterior cranial vault
- lateral orbital margin
- lacrimal bone
- ethmoidal air cell
- zygoma
- maxillary antrum
- mandibular rami

FIGURE 6-15. Facial bones, lateral view, increased rotation.

FACIAL BONES—LATERAL VIEW—COMPARISON STUDY SHOWING INCREASED ROTATION
(Figs. 6-15 and 6-16)

- Increased head rotation will allow the **nasal bones** to be partially visualized, with the **lacrimal bones** superimposed by the upper frontal process of the **zygomatic bone.**

- **Ethmoidal air cell** will show between the **lateral orbital margins.**

- **Maxillary bones** and **antra** are partially obscured by double margins.

- The floor of the **anterior cranial vault** will appear elongated.

- Note the increased distance between the posterior margins of the **mandibular rami.**

CORRECTIVE ADJUSTMENT: Rotate face away from film surface approximately 10 degrees so that the total midsagittal plane is parallel to film surface.

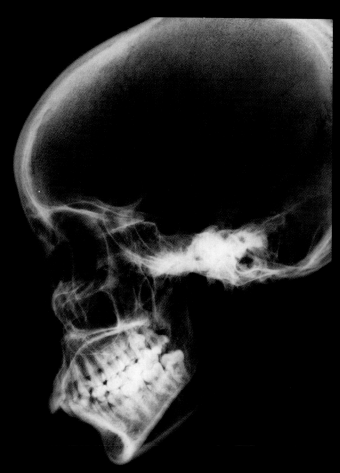

FIGURE 6-16. Facial bones, lateral view, increased rotation.

FACIAL BONES— SUBMENTOVERTICAL VIEW OF ZYGOMATIC ARCHES— ROUTINE
(Figs. 6-17 to 6-20)

PURPOSE. A submentovertical projection to demonstrate the long axis of the bilateral zygomatic arches on a masked film holder.

POSITION. Place the patient in a supine elevated position (6-in. cushion or positioning blocks) or erect posterior position, resting the vertex of the head on a masked film holder or a head unit. If patient is supine, the knees should be flexed to reduce neck strain. Manipulate the head, placing the midsagittal plane perpendicular to, and the infraorbitomeatal line parallel to, the film surface.

PROJECTION. The central ray is projected perpendicular to the infraorbitomeatal line, through a center point in line with the mandibular angles, to the center of the masked film holder.

TIMELY TIPS:

A reverse, unilateral view of the zygomatic arch may be obtained by tilting the vertex of the head away from the arch and aligning a perpendicular tangent from the parietal region to the mandibular ramus.

A nonscreen film holder with screen film will provide less contrast and better definition of the arch.

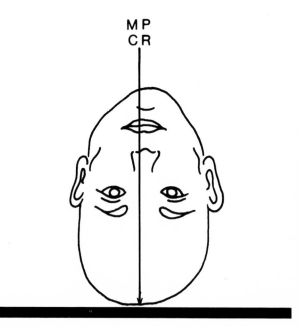

FIGURE 6-17. Facial bones, anterior aspect, submentovertical projection.

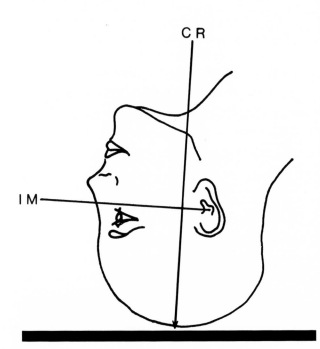

FIGURE 6-18. Facial bones, lateral aspect, submentovertical projection.

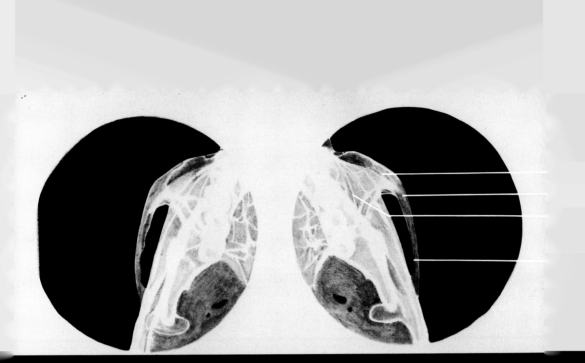

FIGURE 6-19. Facial bones, submentovertical view, routine.

VIEW: ANATOMIC DEMONSTRATION

- Zygomatic arch formed by the **temporal process** of the zygomatic bone and the **zygomatic process** of the temporal bone.

- Zygomatic process of the **maxillary** superimposed over the **body of zygoma.**

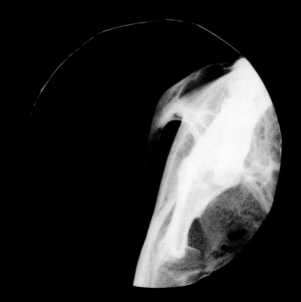
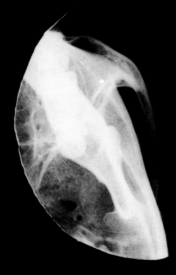

FIGURE 6-20. Facial bones, su tical view, routine.

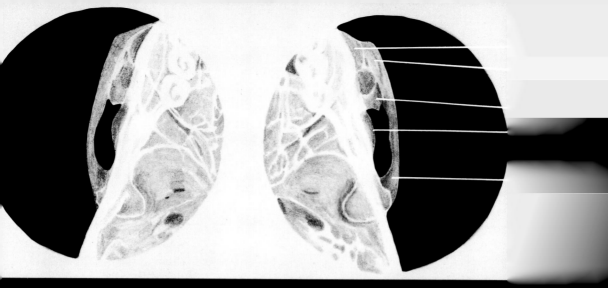

FIGURE 6-21. Facial bones, submentover-tical view, increased extension.

FACIAL BONES— SUBMENTOVERTICAL VIEW OF ZYGOMATIC ARCHES— COMPARISON STUDY SHOWING INCREASED EXTENSION
(Figs. 6-21 and 6-22)

● Increased extension of the neck will show elongation of the zygomatic arches.

● An inferosuperior view o⬛ and **maxillary proces⬛ matic bone,** along with **process** of the **maxilla⬛** seen.

● Note the increase in sp⬛ zygomatic arch and parie⬛

CORRECTIVE ADJUSTM⬛
flexion at the neck 20 degrees⬛

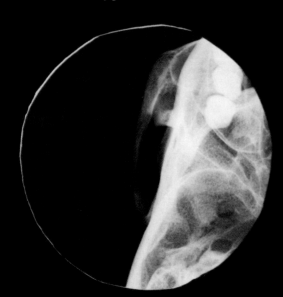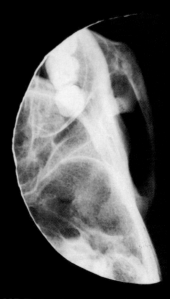

FIGURE 6-22. Facial bones⬛ tical view, increased exten⬛

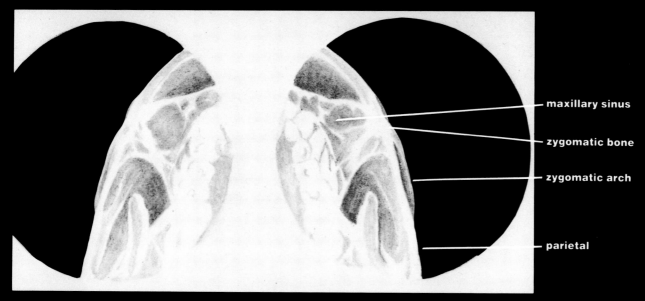

maxillary sinus

zygomatic bone

zygomatic arch

parietal

FIGURE 6-23. Facial bones, submentovertical view, increased flexion.

FACIAL BONES— SUBMENTOVERTICAL VIEW OF ZYGOMATIC ARCHES— COMPARISON STUDY SHOWING INCREASED FLEXION
(Figs. 6-23 and 6-24)

- Increased flexion of the neck will show the **zygomatic arches** nearly obscured by the larger diameter of the **parietal** region.

- The base of the **zygomatic arch** is not visible.

- Note that the space between the **zygomatic arch** and the **parietal** region is no longer visible.

CORRECTIVE ADJUSTMENT: Increase extension at the neck 20 degrees.

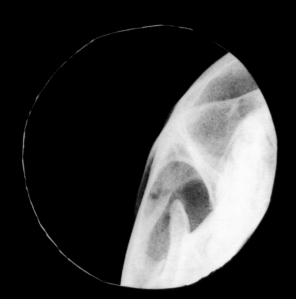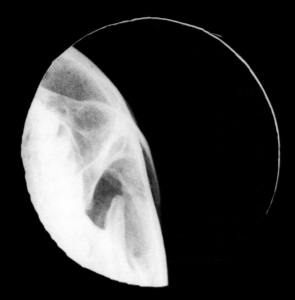

FIGURE 6-24. Facial bones, submentovertical view, increased flexion.

FACIAL BONES—ANTERIOR VIEW OF OPTIC FORAMEN (RHESE)—ROUTINE (Figs. 6-25 to 6-28)

PURPOSE. A posteroanterior projection to demonstrate the optic foramen, open in its fullest diameter, inside the lower, lateral orbital ridge.

POSITION. Place the patient in a prone or erect anterior position, with the midsagittal plane perpendicular to the film holder. Rotate the face 40 degrees away from the orbit being examined. Align the acanthiomeatal line perpendicular to the side of the table or headboard.

PROJECTION. The central ray is projected perpendicularly, through a point inside the lower lateral orbital ridge, to the center of the film holder.

TIMELY TIPS:
Bilateral views of the optic foramina should be taken for comparison studies.

Magnified views of the optic foramina may be obtained with supine patients by reversing the above procedures.

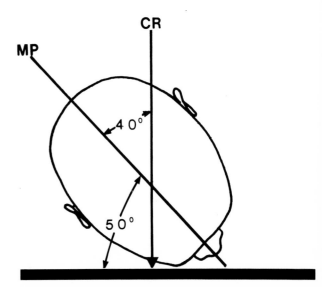

FIGURE 6-25. Facial bones, cranial aspect, axial projection.

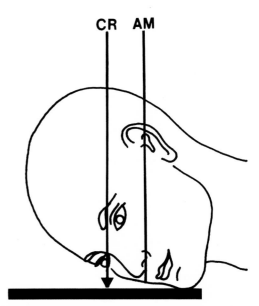

FIGURE 6-26. Facial bones, oblique aspect, axial projection.

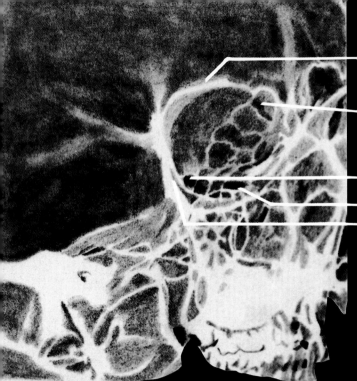

orbital ridge

frontal air cell

optic foramen

ethmoidal air cell

sphenoid ridge

FIGURE 6-27. Facial bones, anterior view of optic foramen, routine.

VIEW: ANATOMIC DEMONSTRATION

- **Optic foramen** located inside the lower, lateral **orbital ridge.**

- **Sphenoid ridge.**

- **Orbital margins** or **ridges.**

- **Ethmoidal air cells** and **frontal air cells.**

- Note the location of the **optic foramen** adjacent to the inner margin of the bony eye orbit.

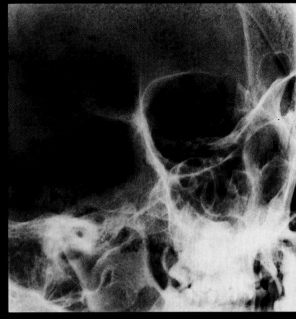

FIGURE 6-28. Facial bones, anterior view of optic foramen, routine.

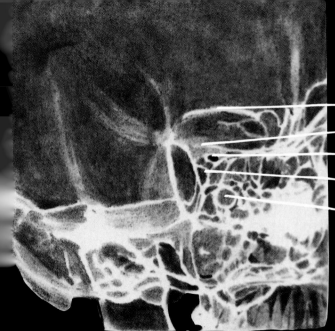
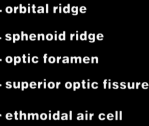

- orbital ridge
- sphenoid ridge
- optic foramen
- superior optic fissure
- ethmoidal air cell

FIGURE 6-29. Facial bones, anterior view of optic foramen, decreased rotation and increased flexion.

FACIAL BONES—ANTERIOR VIEW OF OPTIC FORAMEN— COMPARISON STUDY SHOWING DECREASED ROTATION AND INCREASED FLEXION (Figs. 6-29 and 6-30)

Decreased head rotation and increased flexion will show the **optic foramen** in the upper, medial portion of the orbit, with the diameter of the opening diminished.

The **sphenoid ridge** is shown in the upper level of the orbit.

The inferior portion of the **superior optic fissure** appears below the **optic foramen.**

The **ethmoidal air cells** are shown at an oblique angle.

Note the distance between the **optic foramen** and the lower lateral **orbital ridge.**

CORRECTIVE ADJUSTMENT: Increase rotation 15 degrees and extension 5 degrees.

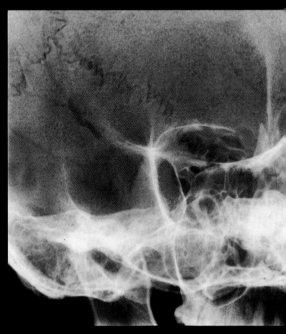

FIGURE 6-30. Facial bones, anterior view of optic foramen, decreased rotation and increased flexion.

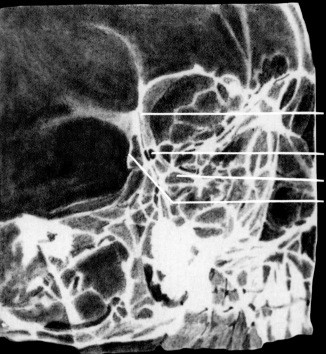

— orbital margin

— optic foramen

— ethmoidal air cell

— sphenoid ridge

FIGURE 6-31. Facial bones, anterior view of optic foramen, increased rotation and increased extension.

FACIAL BONES—ANTERIOR VIEW OF OPTIC FORAMEN— COMPARISON STUDY SHOWING INCREASED ROTATION AND EXTENSION (Figs. 6-31 and 6-32)

- Increased head rotation and extension will show the **optic foramen** superimposed over the lower lateral **orbital margin.**

- The **sphenoid ridge** extends downward across the lower orbital cavity.

- The **ethmoidal air cells** are obscured by the **sphenoid ridge.**

CORRECTIVE ADJUSTMENT: Decrease rotation 5 degrees and increase flexion 5 degrees.

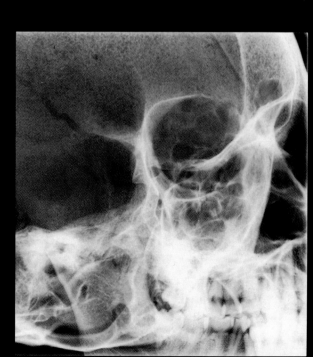

FACIAL BONES—LATERAL VIEW OF NASAL BONES— BILATERAL ROUTINE (Figs. 6-33 to 6-36)

PURPOSE. A lateral projection to demonstrate the nasal bones superimposed.

POSITION. From a prone or erect anterior position, turn the face away from the side being examined, resting the ear against the table or headboard. Rotate the body into an oblique position to ease the strain on the cervical spine. Manipulate the head to place the midsagittal plane parallel, and the interpupillary line perpendicular, to the film surface. Flex the neck so that the canthomeatal line is perpendicular to the side of the table or headboard.

PROJECTION. The central ray is projected perpendicularly, through the nasal bones, to each center of a bilateral, masked cone field.

TIMELY TIPS:

Use of screen film in nonscreen film holder will enhance structural detail.

An axial, superoinferior view may be obtained by placing an occlusal film in the mouth and projecting the central ray in line with the glabelloalveolar line.

Position both sides of the nasal bones for comparison studies.

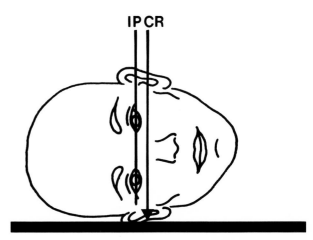

FIGURE 6-33. Facial bones, anterior aspect, lateral projection.

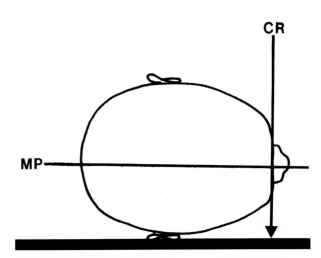

FIGURE 6-34. Facial bones, cranial aspect, lateral projection.

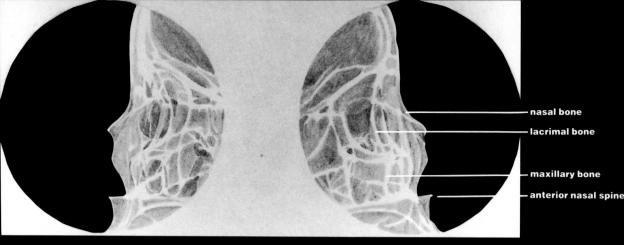

nasal bone
lacrimal bone

maxillary bone
anterior nasal spine

FIGURE 6-35. Facial bones, lateral nasal view, routine.

VIEW: ANATOMIC DEMONSTRATION

- Bilateral **nasal bones** superimposed.

- Frontal processes of **maxillary bones** superimposed.

- **Lacrimal bones** superimposed.

- **Anterior nasal spine.**

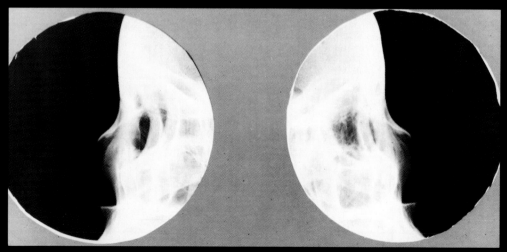

FIGURE 6-36. Facial bones, lateral nasal view, routine.

FACIAL BONES—INFERIOR VIEW OF MAXILLAE—ROUTINE
(Figs. 6-37 to 6-40)

PURPOSE. A superoinferior projection to demonstrate the anterior maxillary region.

POSITION. Place the patient in a supine or erect sitting position. Insert a 2 × 3 in. occlusal film holder in the patient's mouth as far as physically possible. Place the midsagittal plane in line with the central ray projection.

PROJECTION. The central ray is projected 45 degrees away from the glabelloalveolar line, caudally, through the anterior nasal spine to the film holder.

TIMELY TIPS:
The left or right maxillary region may be emphasized by turning the face 35 to 45 degrees away from the side to be examined.

The corner of a nonscreen film holder may be substituted for the occlusal film.

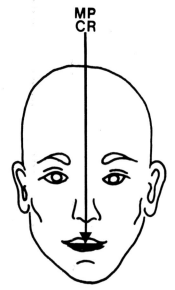

FIGURE 6-37. Facial bones, anterior aspect, superoinferior projection.

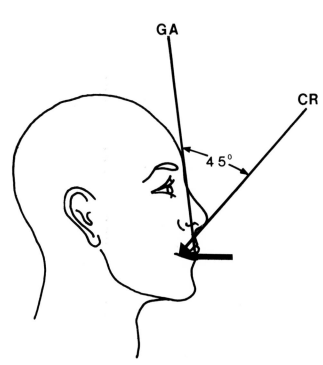

FIGURE 6-38. Facial bones, lateral aspect, superoinferior projection.

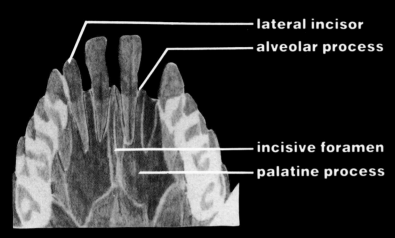

lateral incisor
alveolar process

incisive foramen
palatine process

FIGURE 6-39. Facial bones, inferior maxillary view, routine.

VIEW: ANATOMIC DEMONSTRATION

- Anterior maxillary region.

- Central and **lateral incisors** of maxillary bone with corresponding **alveolar process.**

- Anterior portion of the **palatine processes** of the maxillary bone.

- Region of the **incisive foramen.**

- Note the length of the central incisors.

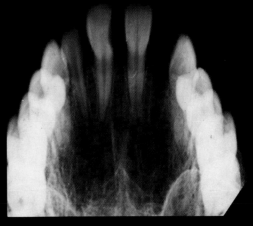

FIGURE 6-40. Facial bones, inferior maxillary view, routine.

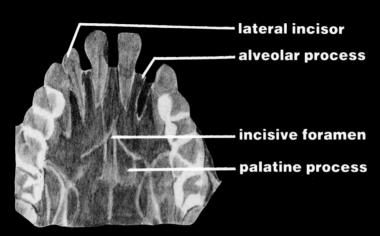

lateral incisor

alveolar process

incisive foramen

palatine process

FIGURE 6-41. Facial bones, inferior view of maxillae, decreased projection.

FACIAL BONES—INFERIOR VIEW OF MAXILLAE— COMPARISON STUDY SHOWING DECREASED PROJECTION (Figs. 6-41 and 6-42)

- Decreased central ray angulation or increased flexion will show the **anterior maxillary region** with fair definition.

- The central and **lateral incisors** will appear foreshortened within the **alveolar process.**

- The anterior portion of the **palatine processes** will be well defined.

- The region of the **incisive foramen** will be better defined.

- Note the length of the incisors in this view compared with the routine view.

CORRECTIVE ADJUSTMENT: Increase central ray angulation **OR** decrease flexion of the neck 10 degrees.

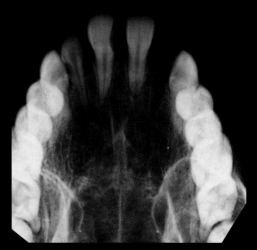

FIGURE 6-42. Facial bones, inferior view of maxillae, decreased projection.

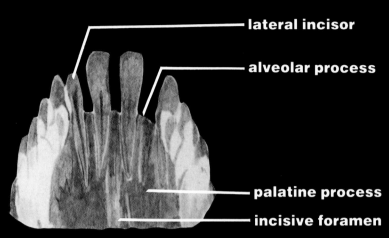

— lateral incisor

— alveolar process

— palatine process

— incisive foramen

FIGURE 6-43. Facial bones, inferior view of maxillae, increased projection.

FACIAL BONES—INFERIOR VIEW OF MAXILLAE—COMPARISON STUDY SHOWING INCREASED PROJECTION
(Figs. 6-43 and 6-44)

- Increased central ray angulation or increased extension will show the anterior maxillary with increased distortion and decreased definition.

- The central and **lateral incisors** will be elongated within the **alveolar process.**

- The anterior portion of the **palatine processes** will show loss of definition through distortion.

- The region of the **incisive foramen** is distorted posteriorly.

- Note the length of the incisors in this view compared with the routine view.

CORRECTIVE ADJUSTMENT: Decreased central ray angulation **OR** extension at the neck 10 degrees.

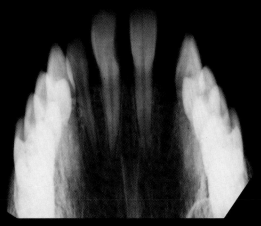

FIGURE 6-44. Facial bones, inferior view of maxillae, increased projection.

FACIAL BONES—LATERAL VIEW OF TEMPOROMANDIBULAR JOINTS—ROUTINE
(Figs. 6-45 to 6-48)

PURPOSE. A lateral projection to show the condyle of the mandible in relation to the mandibular fossa of the temporal bone.

POSITION. From a prone or erect anterior position, turn the face away from the side of the mandible against the table or headboard. Rotate the body into an oblique position to ease the strain on the cervical spine. Manipulate the head to place the midsagittal plane parallel, and the interpupillary line perpendicular, to the film surface. Extend the neck so that the acanthiomeatal line is perpendicular to the side of the table or headboard.

PROJECTION. The central ray is projected 15 degrees caudad, through a point ½ in. anterior to the EAM, on the down side, to the center of the film holder.

TIMELY TIPS:
Bilateral views to include closed and open positions of the mandible are recommended. Insert a sterile cork between the upper and lower incisors to secure the open position.

Positioning accuracy is enhanced when the 15-degree caudal projection is precentered to a selected point on the table; then position the patient directly over the selected point.

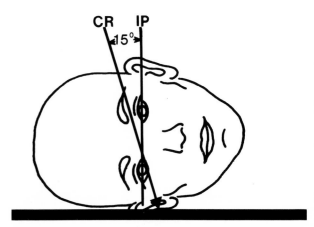

FIGURE 6-45. Facial bones, anterior aspect, lateral projection.

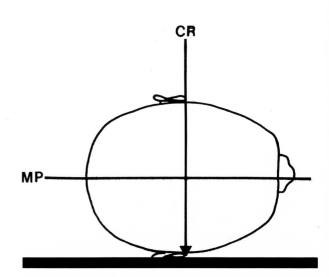

FIGURE 6-46. Facial bones, cranial aspect, lateral projection.

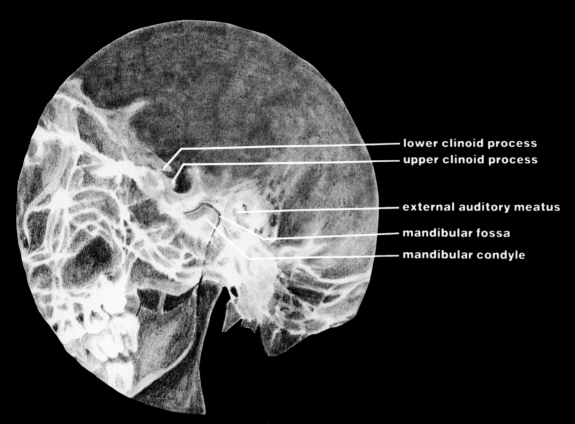

lower clinoid process
upper clinoid process

external auditory meatus
mandibular fossa
mandibular condyle

FIGURE 6-47. Facial bones, temporomandibular joints, lateral closed view, routine.

VIEW: ANATOMIC DEMONSTRATION

- **Mandibular condyle** in relation to its compatible **mandibular fossa.**

- **Upper clinoid processes** projected below the **lower clinoid processes.**

- Elliptical appearance of the adjacent **external auditory meatus.**

- The open-mouth position would show the **mandibular condyle** approximately 1 cm inferior and anterior to the **mandibular fossa.**

- Note the distance between the two mandibular condyles.

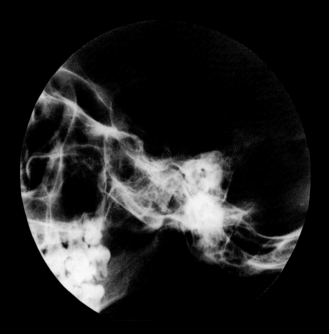

FIGURE 6-48. Facial bones, temporomandibular joints, lateral closed view, routine.

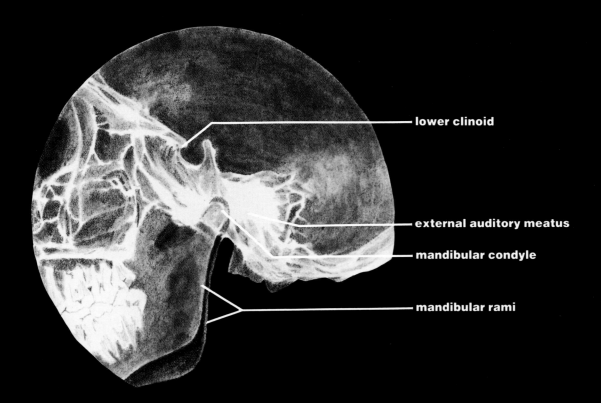

lower clinoid

external auditory meatus

mandibular condyle

mandibular rami

FIGURE 6-49. Facial bones, lateral view of temporomandibular joints, decreased projection.

FACIAL BONES— LATERAL VIEW OF TEMPOROMANDIBULAR JOINTS—COMPARISON STUDY SHOWING DECREASED PROJECTION (Figs. 6-49 and 6-50)

- Decreased central ray angulation or head tilt toward the central ray projection will show near superimposition of the **mandibular condyles.**

- The upper and **lower clinoids** will appear superimposed.

- The regions of the **external auditory meatuses** will appear superimposed.

- Note the close proximity of the **mandibular rami.**

CORRECTIVE ADJUSTMENT: Increase central ray angulation **OR** decrease head tilt 10 degrees.

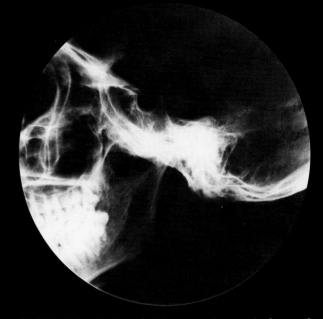

FIGURE 6-50. Facial bones, lateral view of temporomandibular joints, decreased projection.

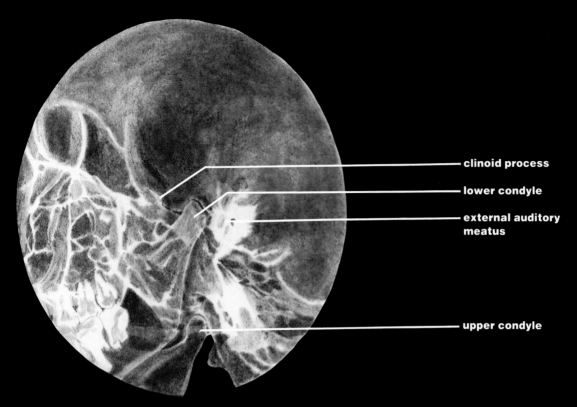

clinoid process

lower condyle

external auditory
meatus

upper condyle

FIGURE 6-51. Facial bones, lateral view of temporomandibular joints, increased projection.

FACIAL BONES— LATERAL VIEW OF TEMPOROMANDIBULAR JOINTS—COMPARISON STUDY SHOWING INCREASED PROJECTION
(Figs. 6-51 and 6-52)

- Increased central ray angulation or increased head tilt away from the central projection will show the **upper condyle** projected far below the **lower condyle** being examined.

- The **clinoid processes** are distorted and projected into underlying structures.

- The region of the **external auditory meatuses** will appear very slightly changed in design although widely separated.

- Note the increased distance between the **mandibular rami.**

CORRECTIVE ADJUSTMENT: Decrease central ray angulation **OR** decrease head tilt 10 degrees.

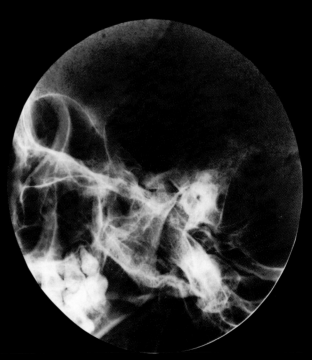

FIGURE 6-52. Facial bones, lateral view of temporomandibular joints, increased projection.

FACIAL BONES—ANTERIOR VIEW OF MANDIBULAR RAMI—ROUTINE
(Figs. 6-53 to 6-56)

PURPOSE. A posteroanterior projection to demonstrate the mandibular rami.

POSITION. Place the patient in a prone or erect anterior position, resting the forehead and nose on the table or headboard. Both the midsagittal plane and canthomeatal line are perpendicular to the film surface. Place the patient's hands by the sides of the head to help stabilize the body.

PROJECTION. The central ray is projected perpendicularly through a point in line with the mandibular angles, to the center of the film holder.

TIMELY TIPS:
For hypersthenic patients with short necks, use a grid cassette placed on top of a support sponge.

For supine patients, reverse procedure and make unilateral exposures with the face rotated 5 degrees away from the side being examined to eliminate superimposition of posterior maxillary region.

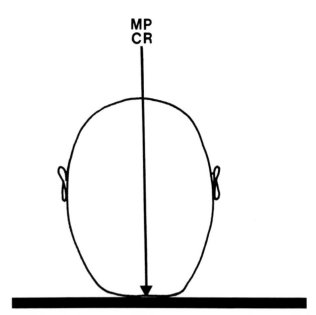

FIGURE 6-53. Facial bones, cranial aspect, posteroanterior projection.

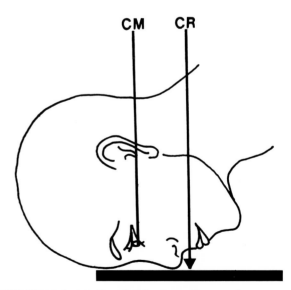

FIGURE 6-54. Facial bones, lateral aspect, posteroanterior projection.

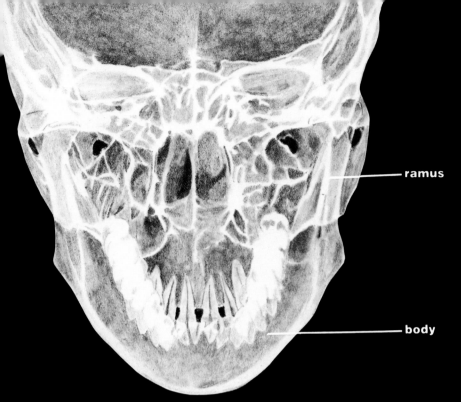

ramus

body

FIGURE 6-55. Facial bones, mandibular rami, anterior view, routine.

VIEW: ANATOMIC DEMONSTRATION

- Mandibular **rami** from each neck to their union with the **mandibular body.**

- The **central body** and mental region will be mostly obscured by the cervical spine.

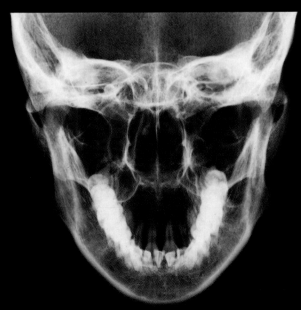

FIGURE 6-56. Facial bones, mandibular rami, anterior view, routine.

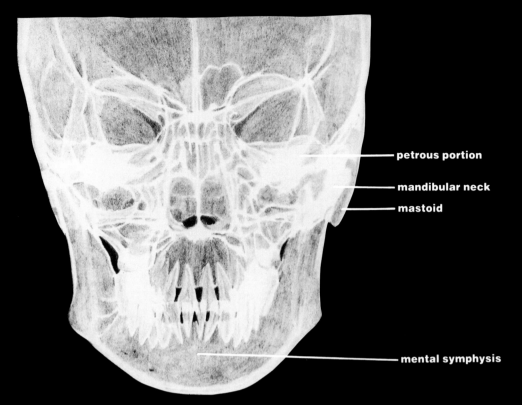

- petrous portion
- mandibular neck
- mastoid
- mental symphysis

FIGURE 6-57. Facial bones, anterior view of mandibular rami, caudal projection.

FACIAL BONES—ANTERIOR VIEW OF MANDIBULAR RAMI—COMPARISON STUDY SHOWING CAUDAL PROJECTION
(Figs. 6-57 and 6-58)

- Caudal central ray angulation or increased extension will show superimposition of the **petrous portion** over the mandibular condyles.

- The posterior base of the occipital bone and **mastoids** will be superimposed over the **mandibular necks.**

- The region of the **mental symphysis** will be demonstrated in a true anterior profile, although it will remain mostly obscured by the cervical spine.

CORRECTIVE ADJUSTMENT: Decrease caudal central ray angulation **OR** increase flexion 10 degrees.

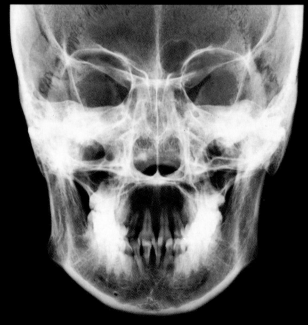

FIGURE 6-58. Facial bones, anterior view of mandibular rami, caudal projection.

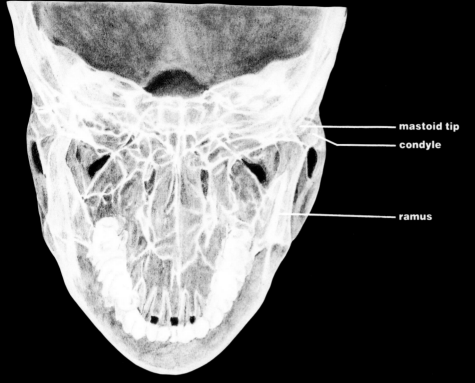

mastoid tip
condyle
ramus

FIGURE 6-59. Facial bones, anterior view of mandibular rami, cephalad projection.

FACIAL BONES—ANTERIOR VIEW OF MANDIBULAR RAMI—COMPARISON STUDY SHOWING CEPHALAD PROJECTION (Figs. 6-59 and 6-60)

- Cephalad central ray angulation or increased flexion will show a full anterior view of the **rami** that is slightly elongated because of divergent ray distortion.

- The **mandibular condyles** will remain partially superimposed by the **mastoid tips** in this closed-mouth position.

CORRECTIVE ADJUSTMENT: Decrease cephalad central ray angulation **OR** increase extension 10 degrees.

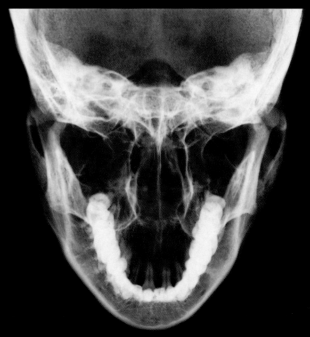

FIGURE 6-60. Facial bones, anterior view of mandibular rami, cephalad projection.

FACIAL BONES—ANTERIOR VIEW OF MANDIBULAR CONDYLES—ROUTINE
(Figs. 6-61 to 6-64)

PURPOSE. A posteroanterior projection to demonstrate the mandibular condyles below the cranial floor.

POSITION. Place the patient in a prone or erect anterior position, resting the forehead and nose on the table or headboard. Both the midsagittal plane and canthomeatal line are perpendicular to the film surface. Place the patient's hands by the sides of the head to help stabilize the body. Just before making the exposure, place a sterile cork between the patient's upper and lower incisors, then re-align the position.

PROJECTION. The central ray is projected 12 degrees cephalad, through the nasion, to the center of the film holder.

TIMELY TIPS:
Minimize prolonged positioning with cork in patient's mouth to reduce discomfort and subsequent motion.

A submentovertical skull position will demonstrate medial displacement of condylar fractures in patients with immobilized mandibles.

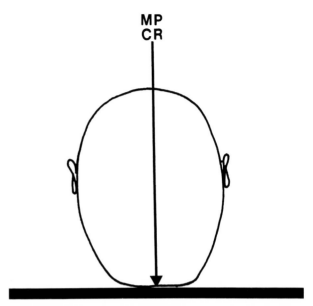

FIGURE 6-61. Facial bones, cranial aspect, posteroanterior projection.

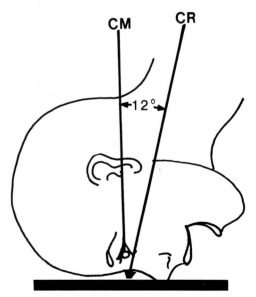

FIGURE 6-62. Facial bones, lateral aspect, posteroanterior projection.

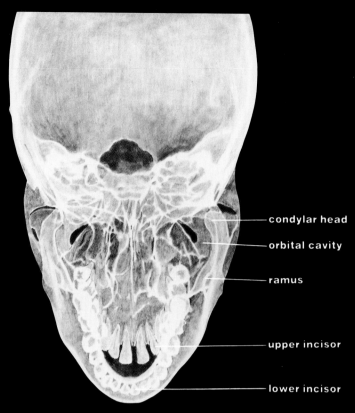

condylar head

orbital cavity

ramus

upper incisor

lower incisor

FIGURE 6-63. Facial bones, mandibular condyle, anterior view, routine.

VIEW: ANATOMIC DEMONSTRATION

- Full anterior view of condylar heads and necks below the temporal base and superimposed over the lateral margins of the **orbital cavities.**

- The **rami** are demonstrated but are somewhat foreshortened because of the central ray angulation.

- Note the distance between the **upper** and **lower incisors.**

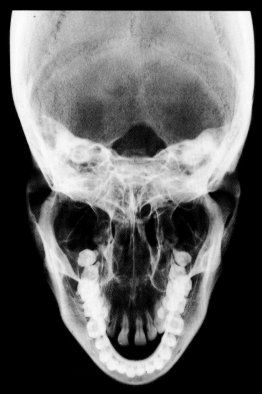

FIGURE 6-64. Facial bones, mandibular condyle, anterior view, routine.

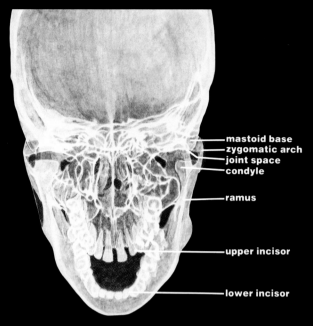

mastoid base
zygomatic arch
joint space
condyle

ramus

upper incisor

lower incisor

FIGURE 6-65. Facial bones, anterior view of mandibular condyles, decreased projection.

FACIAL BONES—ANTERIOR VIEW OF MANDIBULAR CONDYLES—COMPARISON STUDY SHOWING DECREASED PROJECTION (Figs. 6-65 and 6-66)

- Decreased central ray angulation or increased extension will show increased **joint space** between the **mandibular condyles** and corresponding fossae when the mouth is fully opened.

- The **joint spaces** will diminish and be superimposed by the mastoid bases when additional extension or reduction of angulation is incorporated.

- The lateral **mandibular condyles** and necks will be partially obscured by the **zygomatic arches.**

- The **mandibular rami** are well demonstrated.

- Note the increased distance between the **upper** and **lower incisors** resulting from more direct divergent ray projection.

CORRECTIVE ADJUSTMENT: Increase central ray angulation **OR** flexion 10 degrees.

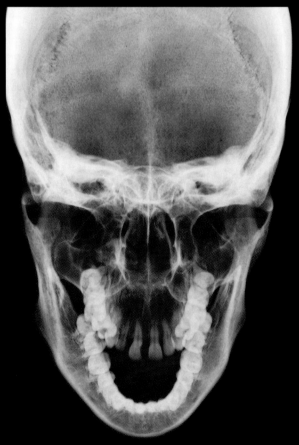

FIGURE 6-66. Facial bones, anterior view of mandibular condyles, decreased projection.

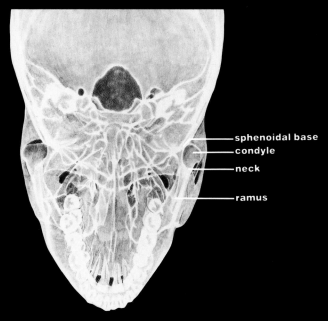

FIGURE 6-67. Facial bones, anterior view of mandibular condyles, increased projection.

FACIAL BONES—ANTERIOR VIEW OF MANDIBULAR CONDYLES—COMPARISON STUDY SHOWING INCREASED PROJECTION
(Figs. 6-67 and 6-68)

- Increased central ray angulation or increased flexion will show the **condyles** superimposed into the temporal and **sphenoidal bases.**

- The **mandibular necks** and **rami** will appear foreshortened.

- The mandibular bodies will appear narrowed because of the increased cephalic projection and remain mostly obscured by the cervical spine.

- By converting to occipital-skull technique, this position (HAAS) may be used as a reverse occipital projection to demonstrate the petrous portion, foramen magnum, and occipital bone.

- Note the superimposition of the lower over the upper teeth.

CORRECTIVE ADJUSTMENT: Decrease central ray angulation **OR** flexion 10 degrees.

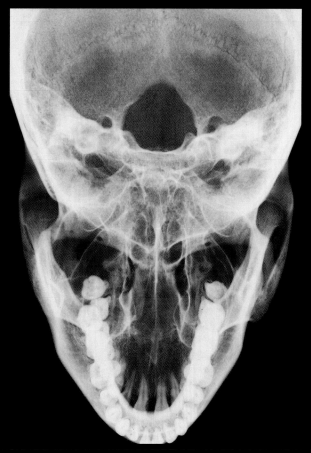

FIGURE 6-68. Facial bones, anterior view of mandibular condyles, increased projection.

FACIAL BONES—LATERAL VIEW OF MANDIBLE—ROUTINE
(Figs. 6-69 to 6-72)

PURPOSE. A mediolateral projection to demonstrate the mandibular rami and posterior body.

POSITION. Place the patient in an erect, semi-anterior oblique position, resting the parietal eminence against the headboard or film holder. With the patient's thoracic spine as straight as possible and the shoulders relaxed, extend the chin forward, aligning the long axis of the inferior mandibular ramus and posterior body parallel to both the film surface and the floor. The head is tilted 25 degrees toward the film holder.

PROJECTION. The central ray is projected horizontally and perpendicularly, through the inferior ramus, to the center of the film holder.

TIMELY TIPS:
Lateral, nongrid, cervical spine technique will provide excellent visibility.

Make exposure 3 sec after complete suspended *EXPIRATION* to help reduce motion.

Extension of the chin is important to preclude superimposition of the cervical spine over the posterior ramus.

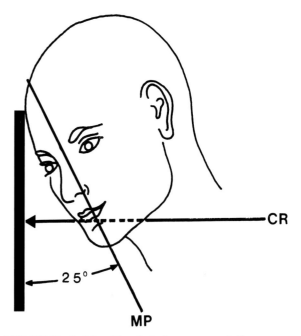

FIGURE 6-69. Facial bones, oblique aspect, mediolateral projection.

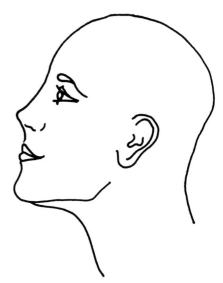

FIGURE 6-70. Facial bones, lateral aspect, mediolateral projection.

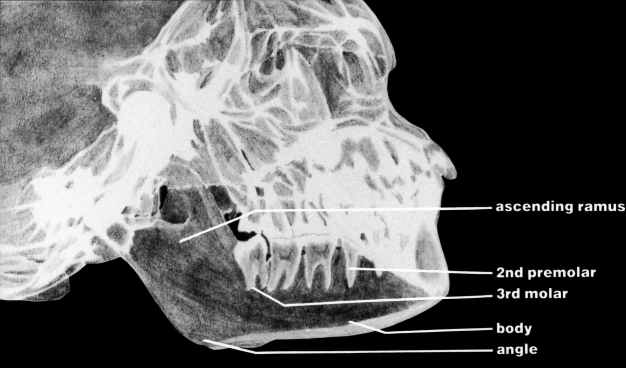

ascending ramus

2nd premolar

3rd molar

body

angle

FIGURE 6-71. Facial bones, lateral mandibular view, routine.

VIEW: ANATOMIC DEMONSTRATION

- Lateral **ascending ramus.**

- Inferior ramus and posterior **mandibular body** to the level of the **second premolar.**

- **First, second,** and **third molars.**

- **Mandibular angle.**

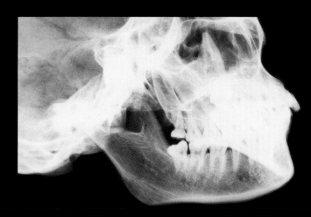

FIGURE 6-72. Facial bones, lateral mandibular view, routine.

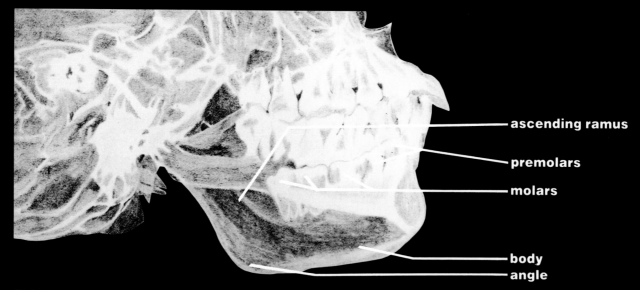

ascending ramus

premolars

molars

body
angle

FIGURE 6-73. Facial bones, lateral view of mandible, decreased rotation.

FACIAL BONES—LATERAL VIEW OF MANDIBLE—COMPARISON STUDY SHOWING DECREASED ROTATION
(Figs. 6-73 and 6-74)

- Decreased head rotation will show superimposition of the **ascending mandibular rami.**

- Superimposition of the upper **mandibular body** over the **premolars** and **molars.**

- The **mandibular angle** is well visualized.

CORRECTIVE ADJUSTMENT: Increase head rotation (face toward the film holder) 10 degrees.

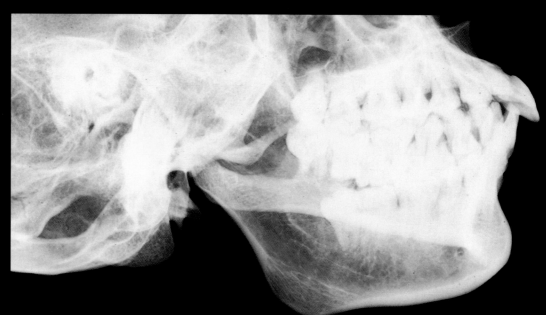

FIGURE 6-74. Facial bones, lateral view of mandible, decreased rotation.

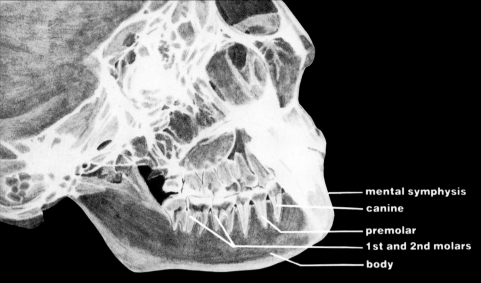

mental symphysis
canine
premolar
1st and 2nd molars
body

FIGURE 6-75. Facial bones, lateral view of mandible, increased rotation and increased tilt.

FACIAL BONES—LATERAL VIEW OF MANDIBLE— COMPARISON STUDY SHOWING INCREASED ROTATION AND TILT (Figs. 6-75 and 6-76)

- Increased head rotation and tilt will show the ascending ramus slightly distorted in height and width.

- The inferior ramus and posterior **body** are fully visualized, to the level of the **canine tooth,** with slight elongation toward the anterior portion.

- The **molars** are foreshortened in height.

- The **mandibular angle** is well visualized.

CORRECTIVE ADJUSTMENT: Decrease both head tilt and rotation 10 degrees.

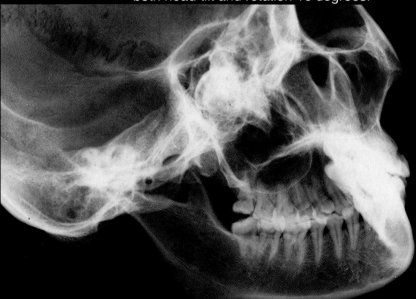

FIGURE 6-76. Facial bones, lateral view of mandible, increased rotation and increased tilt.

FACIAL BONES— SUBMENTOVERTICAL VIEW OF MANDIBULAR BODIES AND SYMPHYSIS—ROUTINE
(Figs. 6-77 to 6-80)

PURPOSE. A submentovertical projection to demonstrate the anterior mandibular body and symphysis and their respective teeth.

POSITION. Place the patient in a supine or erect posterior position with the vertex of the head resting against the table top or headboard. If the patient is supine, elevate the body to ease strain on the cervical spine. Insert an occlusal film holder between the upper and lower teeth.

PROJECTION. The central ray is projected perpendicularly, through the mental point, to the film surface.

TIMELY TIPS:
Screen film or nonscreen film in a plastic film holder may be used in place of occlusal film packets.

For an alternate position, seat patient at end of table, resting on elbows with chin resting on fists. Place film beneath anterior mandible; then project central ray 45 degrees from vertical, through mental symphysis, to film surface.

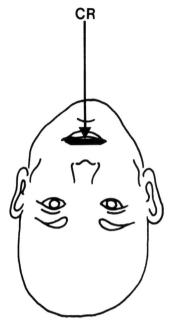

FIGURE 6-77. Facial bones, anterior aspect, submentovertical projection.

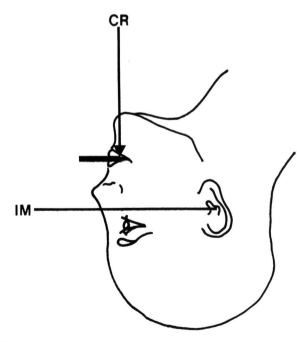

FIGURE 6-78. Facial bones, lateral aspect, submentovertical projection.

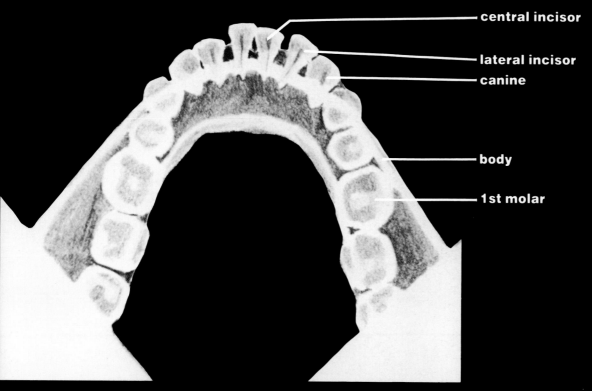

FIGURE 6-79. Facial bones, submentover-tical mandibular view, routine.

VIEW: ANATOMIC DEMONSTRATION

- **Anterior mandibular bodies** and mental symphysis.

- **Central** and **lateral incisors, canines, premolars,** and first and second **molars.**

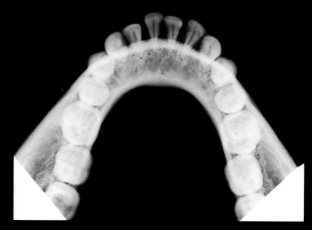

FIGURE 6-80. Facial bones, submentover-tical mandibular view, routine.

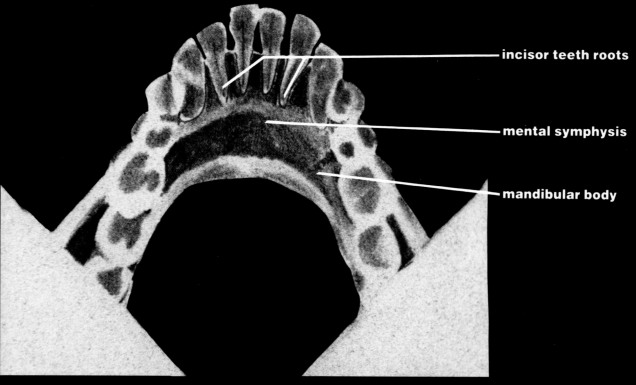

incisor teeth roots

mental symphysis

mandibular body

FIGURE 6-81. Facial bones, submentovertical view of mandibular bodies and symphysis, increased projection.

FACIAL BONES— SUBMENTOVERTICAL VIEW OF MANDIBULAR BODIES AND SYMPHYSIS— COMPARISON STUDY SHOWING INCREASED CAUDAL PROJECTION
(Figs. 6-81 and 6-82)

- Increased caudal central ray angulation or flexion will show the anterior **mandibular bodies** with corresponding tooth crowns elongated.

- The **mental symphysis** region with corresponding teeth will appear elongated with better visibility of the **incisor teeth roots.**

- *Note:* This view is commonly preferred to demonstrate vertical or linear fractures through the **mandibular symphysis.**

CORRECTIVE ADJUSTMENT: Decrease caudal central angulation **OR** flexion 20 degrees.

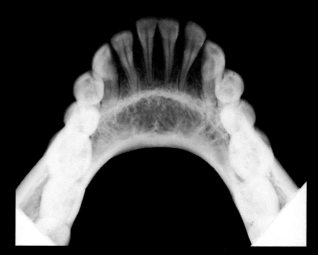

FIGURE 6-82. Facial bones, submentovertical view of mandibular bodies and symphysis, increased projection.

BIBLIOGRAPHY

JACOBI, CA AND PARIS, DQ: *Textbook of Radiologic Technology,* ed 6. CV Mosby, St. Louis, 1977.

MERRILL, V: *Atlas of Roentgenographic Positions and Standard Radiologic Procedures, Vol 2,* ed 4. CV Mosby, St. Louis, 1975.

MESCHAN, I: *An Atlas of Anatomy Basic to Radiology.* WB Saunders, Philadelphia, 1975.

INDEX